the ANXIOUS BREAKUP Journal

by Ben Ihn

Copyright © 2024 by Ben Ihn
All rights reserved.
Published and printed in Canada.

This book is the property of Ben Ihn. No part of this book may be reproduced, stored within a retrieval system, or transmitted in any form or by any means without the author's written permission except for the use of quotations in a book review.

Art by Ben Ihn Copyright © 2024

Cover and interior design by James Warwood
www.cjwarwood.com

Editorial services by Sage Taylor Kingsley
www.SageforYourPage.com

Hardcover ISBN: 9798883496799
Paperback ISBN: 9798863325491

Independently published

Ben Ihn
benjaminihn10@gmail.com
Instagram: soju_knows
Tiktok: soju_knows

TABLE OF CONTENTS

INTRODUCTION...   PG 6

THE RIGHT AFTER...   PG 17
THE HURTING...   PG 53
THE DISCOVERING...   PG 151
THE HEALING...   PG 175

ABOUT THE AUTHOR...   PG 203

. . . Healing takes time

Introduction

Hi,

How the heck are ya?

Actually, don't answer that. I'm gonna take a guess based on the fact that you're here reading this right now. It probably hasn't been easy trying to process everything that's happened as of late. It's not every day you get your heart broken. And when I say "broken"... I mean *broken*. As in: shattered, ripped out, torn to pieces, thrown in the dumpster, shoot me in the face, fuck-my-life "broken."

Trust me: I've been there more times than I'd like to admit.

There are so many emotions probably raging through your head right now: grief, anger, guilt, regret, pain, frustration, confusion, loneliness, anxiousness, emptiness, to name a few (OK, a lot). But if there's one thing I want you to know, it's that you're not alone.

Turns to camera #2

Every day, millions of people across the globe are suffering from a devastating condition known as heartbreak, wondering how they ended up here, how they're going to keep it together at work tomorrow, what they're going to tell their friends and family, and wishing it were all just a terrible dream. Coming to the realization that the person they envisioned spending the rest of their life with is no longer part of their life at all (sheesh, that escalated quickly).

OK, so I have some good news and some bad news for you. Let's start with the bad news.

Ready... ?

The bad news is that if your heart truly is broken, it's not going to be a quick and easy road to recovery. But you already knew that, so this isn't really news to you at all (phew!). You're going to experience a roller coaster of emotions during this next phase of your life.

How long will this shit take, you ask? Well, to be honest, I don't have the answer to that. It could be anywhere from a couple months, to several years (wait, what?). OK. Relax, it probably won't take that long. It's all really dependent on you. And luckily, you've got this book to help you get through the shitty part way faster.

Fair warning, some of your good days will quickly become overshadowed by a stretch of awful ones. There will be days when you don't want to do anything. Days when you just want to give up because it feels like there's literally no point. Days when your heart hurts so much that you feel physically sick to your stomach and can barely eat. Days when you toss and turn in bed for hours, unable to get a wink of sleep, and other days when sleep is the *only* thing you can do.

Days when you feel like there isn't a soul in the world who understands what you're going through. And that's a fact; no one will *ever* truly comprehend the weight of what's happening to you. Because none of them lived it. That's unique to you (you're special like that).

And now for the good news.

Ready... ?

The good news is that just as there are millions of *hopeful* romantics around the world suffering from heartbreak every single day, there are just as many people healing and falling in love all over again.

And so will you.

Yes—you read that right. As much as you're probably utterly disgusted by the idea of falling in love again, unless you want to live in complete solitude with some Buddhist monks in Tibet for the rest of your life, you *will* fall in love again, someday. But let me clarify just so we're on the same page.

Turns back to camera #1

You know what really grinds my gears? People who jump right back into a new relationship immediately after a bad breakup. Why would you commit such a senseless act? The truth is, jumping right back into another premature relationship is probably one of the worst things you can do after getting your heart broken. It's too damn soon. Your heart has just been severely injured, and it needs time to heal. You need to rehab that shit until you're 100% ready to jump back into the game. Rushing these kinds of things can have serious consequences. The example I like to use is Kevin Durant in Game 5 of the 2019 NBA finals vs. the Toronto Raptors. (Yeah, that was five years ago, and us Raptors fans are still riding that wave). Long story short: KD should not have been on the court given the condition of his Achilles before the game. He had a pre-existing injury, everyone knew it, he rushed back to play, and BAM! Tears his Achilles, one of the most difficult injuries for athletes to bounce back from.

But I digress. What these people are really doing is opting for the path of least resistance, placing their source of happiness and self-love in another entity. What they've failed to realize is that those things need to come from within *points to heart*. Yeah, I know that sounds cliché. But hey, it's the truth.

P.S. Since we're on the subject, you should know that this whole thing is going to be a deeply personal and sensitive experience, and at times, it's gonna get a little cheesy, corny, icky, all of the above. So, let's free our minds to be as open and honest as possible. There will be a lot of time for self-reflection. In these moments, you'll have to be honest with yourself and dive deep into exploring your emotions. Besides, it's just you and me here, so don't be shy *wink*.

So, when I say you're going to fall in love again, I mean you're going to fall in love with *yourself* first and foremost before you even think about dating.

That way, when you do eventually meet the right person (or *a* right person), you'll be ready. Your heart will be so full of self-love, confidence, positivity, sexiness, and Big-Dick Energy that you'll literally be dripping in the aura of the unspoken rizz-God. Why? Because despite how you might feel at this moment, you are a star, and you light up the lives of everyone who's blessed enough to be around you. And you're not going to let this one moment stop you from shining bright like a motha fuckin' diamond. @badgalriri

Over the next little while, we're gonna be the best of besties. And like any bestie, I promise I'll be here for you whenever you need me. I'm going to guide you through this process, and we're going to get through this whole thing together—from the initial stage right after the breakup (this part sucks ass), to the hurting (this part sucks even more), to the discovering (this is where it gets good), to finally, the healing (it's fuckin' amazing).

Here's how it works:

I want you to flip through each page chronologically; don't skip pages even if you're in a totally different mental or emotional space than the book. <u>*Do every single exercise*</u>, 'cause it's all important. It's up to you how many pages to do each day, but all I ask is that you flip through at least two to three pages per day. Cool? Cool *dap*.

One last thing. I need you to really commit yourself to this. *Trust the process* because it's not going to be easy; nor will it be a linear path. There may be setbacks along the way, and that's OK. Sometimes you're going to feel like you're going backwards. You're going to have those days where you'd rather just lie in bed and cry all day. Those days are important too. But whenever you fall down, you have to will yourself to get back up and keep pushing forward, because *you* are ultimately the only person who's going to get *you* through this. The world is going to keep moving, with or without you. So, everything is in your hands.

You fucking got this

A LITTLE ABOUT ME . . .

So why the hell should you trust *me* of all people? Seriously, who do I think I am?

Well, my first answer would be, I'm nobody. I'm not a psychologist, counsellor, or therapist. I'm not professionally trained or educated in the cognitive neuroscience behind love or heartbreak. And guess what? I think that makes me the perfect candidate to guide you through this. I'm just a regular dude who happens to have gone through his fair share of heartbreak. And I'm not going to sugarcoat anything. I know firsthand how hard it is, and I know how much adversity you're going to have to face to get through it. In fact, I started writing this book at the peak of my heartbreak. I know it'll help you because everything in here helped me too.

Oh, yeah, I forgot to mention, I'm anxious as FUCK (hooray). For as long as I can remember, I've always had an extremely anxious personality. I overthink everything: what people think about me, my career, my finances, my physical appearance, my relationships with friends and family—the list goes on. Growing up, I was always known as the sensitive and emotional kid. I just accepted it. But I couldn't understand why I had such a hard time dealing with shit, while others appeared to remain completely unfazed by life's hardships. At every stage of my life, I always seemed to be going through an internal battle with myself. I've always been both my staunchest ally and harshest critic.

A few years ago, my 83-year-old therapist told me that I had some of the worst anxiety he'd ever seen in his entire career. Holy shit, my man lived through World War II, Vietnam, Ebola, early 2000s hip-hop fashion, and somehow *I* was one of his worst cases.

How, Sway!? How!?

Needless to say, my anxiety has transcended many forms throughout my life, from panic attacks and social phobias to addiction and clinical depression. Suffering from mental health issues is bad enough. But when you throw heartbreak into the mix, my GOD, that shit is like dropping a nuclear bomb over a blazing wildfire. It's one of the most difficult things I've ever had to overcome in my life.

Like me, someone's who's anxious and heartbroken will meticulously reflect on every single moment throughout the relationship. Every conversation, every interaction, every time you made love, every fight, every beautiful moment, and every moment that left you feeling unworthy.

But it's not just living in the past that really mindfucks an anxious person. It's the deep-rooted fear of what lies ahead, and the incessant paranoia of getting hurt again. We develop trust issues, an irrational fear of abandonment and betrayal, and an unrealistic expectation for others to empathize with our suffering. All our thoughts and emotions become amplified—in all the wrong ways.

I feel incredibly blessed to have had many amazing women come in and out of my life. At age 33, I've been in three serious, long-term relationships; a bunch of not-so-serious ones; and a handful of situationships in between. And no, that's not me flexing. The truth is, relationships were always a means through which I coped with my insecurities. I felt validated whenever I was in one. Like, "yeah, I'm loveable… Right?" The result was I fucked up (most of) those relationships and hurt a lot of people along the way; Most of all, myself.

But each and every relationship, regardless of its outcome, left a lasting imprint on the person I am today and the type of partner I strive to be.

I'm a lover. Always have been, always will be. I love to love, pretty much to a fault. Love has brought me some of the purest forms of joy I've ever experienced in my entire life. Every time I've fallen for someone, I've done everything in my power to fight for that love, to nurture it, and to protect it.

But like anything that has the power to bring happiness, love has the power to bring tragedy, immense pain, and suffering. In my last relationship, I was 100% committed (naively) to the idea that she was the one I was destined to spend the rest of my life with (oh boy, was I wrong). For the first two years of that relationship, I worked my ass off and pushed myself to my limits until I could finally afford a ring that I deemed worthy. I had plans to propose in the Summer of 2021.

But life had plans of its own, things didn't work out as I'd envisioned, and I fell flat on my face. I felt utterly defeated. Despite what they all say, heartbreak does NOT get any easier the more you do it. Your heart never breaks the same way. Each time, it tears open new parts of you that you never knew existed.

So, there I was at 30 years old in the midst of the most agonizing breakup of my life, when a snowball of mental-health issues quickly took over my entire existence. I felt like I was slowly dying from the inside. I was tired of waking up and getting out of bed every day to face a day that felt hopeless. No matter how hard I tried, I couldn't shake off all the pain I was feeling.

I wasn't just emotionally hurt; I was embarrassed and traumatized from the whole experience. There were many times when I thought about un-aliving myself just to put me out of my misery.

One time I came dangerously close and ended up somewhere I shouldn't have been.

But thankfully, something (or someone) inside me screamed, "Ben, what the actual FUCK are you doing? Go home, you idiot.." So, I went home. I don't consider myself a very spiritual person, but I know there was some divine intervention at work that day, and for that I'm truly grateful.

That's what heartbreak can do to you. It completely highjacks your brain and takes you to some of the darkest places you never thought you'd ever go. It can change your whole perspective on life and whether you even want to continue doing it.

Or... it can do something magical

Over three years later, my healing journey continues. I've gone through the ultimate highs and lows that one can feel when going through something as deep of a loss as heartbreak. But the topic of heartbreak, just like mental health, is still such a taboo subject to talk about and share publicly, especially as a man.

There will always be those dusty, Andrew Tate meat-riding incels who are quick to judge and label a heartbroken person as soft, dramatic, and emotional. Um, yeah bitch, I'm emotional right now, so what? Overcoming heartbreak is one of the hardest, most painful—yet bravest and most badass—things you'll ever do in your life.

But it's kinda messed up that we're expected to do it in complete solitude, locked away in our dungeons/bedrooms, pretending everything is fine. How are we supposed to pretend everything is fine when in essence, the most important person in our entire world basically just DIED? (not literally, but you know what I mean.)

So, what was the turning point? What was the secret *sowce* that enabled me to recover?

Well for starters, there was none. There wasn't a single "turning point" or moment where I woke up one day and decided to fix my shit and get over it. Every day was a constant battle of small wins, small reasons to keep going and believe that I had something good coming my way. Each day, I focused on improving a different aspect of myself, including my physical and mental health, my personal relationships, and my self-image and confidence.

As the tiny microfibers in my heart began to repair themselves, I started feeling better too. I thought less about her, and more about me. I started to feel like myself again. I reconnected with old friends, I picked up new hobbies, I got a new job, I bought my first condo (I took the money that I saved for the ring and put it towards a down payment—that's called *lemonade*). And for the first time in a very long time, I started to enjoy life again.

This is how I know you're going to get through this. This is how you heal. And if I can do it, BITCH, so can you.

It was ultimately my closest friends who got me through the darkest period of my life. Having that supportive outlet where I could vent and make sense of all my emotions gave me the therapy and clarity I needed. But even your closest friends have their own lives too. They can't be there for you 24/7, nor should you expect them to be. The reality is, no matter how amazing your support circle is, most of the healing process is spent alone with just you and your thoughts. This time alone can be a great opportunity for self-reflection and healing.

But if you're an anxious piece of shit like me, this time alone can turn you into your worst enemy. If you don't have some structure to calm your ass down and rationalize your thoughts, it can fuck you up. In my case, it *really* fucked me up. Heartbreak is a real bitch, and she will manipulate the shit out of you.

That's why I created this daily journal—to help those who may not always have someone to listen to them in their darkest hours (and because I'm broke af and can't afford therapy). All the questions and reflections in this journal were inspired by real conversations, people, and exercises that helped me during my healing journey. I know that they'll help you too.

So, friend, there are two things that I can guarantee you:

1) *You will get through this.* And no matter how bad it gets, I'll be here for you every step of the way.

2) *This breakup will change you*—in a good way, of course. It will change the essence of who you are. The memories of your ex will always stay with you and have a profound influence on the person you will eventually become. And what I can 100% guarantee is that *you will come out of this a better person* (all because of me—kidding, but not really). This will be one of the most transformational periods of your entire life, so get ready.

Life has so much more in store for you. Hang in there. It gets better, I promise.

So ... do you trust me? *I'm Aladdin, you're Jasmine*

Then hop on this magic carpet, cause we're going for a little ride.

Let's fuckin' go

Time out first
on a serious note ...

I know this is hard. I know that feeling of not wanting to keep going. Trust me, I've been there.

If it ever gets to a point where you're having serious and/or recurrent thoughts about harming yourself (or someone else), please seek help. Remember that you are NEVER alone in this. This too shall pass.

Don't give up

Crisis Services Canada
Call/Text: 988
www.crisisservicescanada.ca

The 988 Suicide and Crisis Lifeline (US)
Call/Text: 988
https://988lifeline.org/

THE RIGHT AFTER

❝
As I walked away,

I PAUSED AND LOOKED BACK...

...TO SEE IF SHE WOULD, TOO.

But she was already gone.

❞

*S*TEP ONE:
take a deep breath, then take another one

This chapter is all about reflection and introspection during the immediate aftermath of the breakup. Your mind might find itself in this weird state of confusion and shock—almost a little numb. On one hand you're like, "Um, what the fuck? Did that really just happen?" and on the other hand you're like,

"Holy fucking shit, that just happened."

This is completely normal. Your brain is still trying to process. Maybe the reality of the situation hasn't even hit you yet (not to freak you out, but it eventually hits you like a truck), so it's important to ground yourself and prepare for whatever emotions come next.

If it's already hit you and you're really feeling that shit, perfect. Hurts like a bitch, doesn't it?

Let's talk about it

THE FIRST MOMENT
immediately after a breakup . . .

I never got used to the feeling. You're either driving away, hopping out of a car, or hanging up the phone, and all of a sudden there's this eerie silence, as if time itself has stopped and you're the last living soul on the planet. It is the loudest silence I've ever heard in my life.

The best way I can describe it is like in war movies when an explosion goes off right beside the guy. He gets the wind knocked out of him and violently thrown to the ground. He trembles as he looks up in a daze and sees chaos and destruction around him, yet all he can hear is a deafening silence and the sound of his heart pounding in his chest. He can see people screaming, trying to get his attention, but he can't hear a single word they're saying as their voices drift off into the void. He just sits there completely helpless, without a clue of what to do next or how to help himself.

Suddenly, an echoing muzzled voice breaks through the haze, pulling you back to reality,

"Bitch! Snap out of it and get your shit together!"

(P.S. the voice is me)

Grab a pen because we're divin' in. I got you.

What's one thing that would make you happy in this moment?

Why?

If happiness seems like a pipe dream, what would at least help you feel a little better?

STEP TWO:
Say hello to the emotional shitstorm

In the space below, write down 20 emotions you're feeling right now. No censoring. Just write down whatever comes out.

#1: _____ #11: _____

#2: _____ #12: _____

#3: _____ #13: _____

#4: _____ #14: _____

#5: _____ #15: _____

#6: _____ #16: _____

#7: _____ #17: _____

#8: _____ #18: _____

#9: _____ #19: _____

#10: _____ #20: _____

It's a lot of emotions all at once, isn't it? So many feels. It's probably a little overwhelming to see them all written out like this. So, close your eyes.

No wait... read this first, then close your eyes:

Take a moment to just be present with all of these emotions, the good and the bad. Imagine yourself doing butterflies in a giant pile of colourful emotional energy. Each colour represents one of the emotions you wrote down. The intensity of these emotions will change constantly. Some will feel like a knife in your back. Some will be circling in front of you, on top of you, and beneath you. Some will disappear and then find their way back into the pile. Whatever you see or hear or sense when you do this is totally fine.

Whenever you feel overwhelmed, grant yourself this gift: pause, close your eyes, take a *deep* breath, and remind yourself that every ounce of discomfort—the confusion, the anxiety, the grief, the pain, the fear—all of it is part of the healing process, and *it's all temporary*. At this moment, you can't make anything disappear, and to try and do so will only invite more suffering into your life.

So let go, free yourself from any desire for control, and just acknowledge this beautiful pile of emotional shit that you're in.

How long has it been since the breakup?

_____ months

_____ days

_____ hours

(Btw, "6, 8, 12," by Brian McKnight. Shoutout to all my millennials. IYKYK)

When was the first moment you realized it, and what did that feel like?

_____

_____

_____

_____

_____

_____

_____

_____

_____

_____

_____

_____

_____

_____

WAKING UP
to no "Good Morning" text

This is usually when it really fuckin' hits you. How could it not? It was the one thing you did consistently with your partner every single day. Saying good morning and good night to them was a daily routine. All of a sudden, that 3-second part of your day is gone, but those 3 seconds meant everything. It's truly one of the most gut-wrenching feelings in the world; checking your phone first thing in the morning and seeing that blank screen; one that would have normally been occupied with the most beautiful good morning text that you'd probably do anything to receive now.

It's amazing how the removal of such a seemingly small act can be so devastating. But it makes sense. Because it was that one thing— the first thing in fact, that reminded you every single morning, "Our two spirits are intertwined, and no matter how brutal your day is looking and whatever bullshit you got going on, don't forget: I love you, and I'm thinking about you. And at the end of this day, I'll still love you and be here waiting for you."

Like damn, who wouldn't miss that?

No matter what I say, that feeling of checking your phone and being reminded you're single is always going to suck. But you have to keep reminding yourself that this is all an inherent part of the healing process. As you journey forward, you'll continue to encounter many more moments like this, and it'll always be a bit of an emotional battle. It will feel extremely uncomfortable because you're not used to having to seize each day independently, even if you didn't live together. You grew accustomed to being part of a team. You're flying solo now, and it feels like a void or a vacuum. Be present in these feelings. Don't run from them; it's OK to grieve.

I promise you will get through it as long as you keep believing you will.

Take a deep breath, close your eyes,
and repeat after me:

"NO MATTER HOW BAD IT GETS . . .

. . . I WILL GET THROUGH THIS."

Say it out loud 20 times.
Nice and slow.
Breathe all the way in and out between each one.

ON CONTROL...

By now you're probably feeling pretty anxious. So many thoughts and feelings all at once, it's just a big clusterfuck of questions with no answers.

What's my ex thinking?

What are they doing right now?

Are they already messaging, dating, or fucking someone else?

What are they saying to other people?

What am I going to tell my friends and family, and when?

What about that wedding / concert / trip we had planned?

What about the stuff I left at their house / stuff they left at my house?

Who's going to take my side?

Who's going to take their side?

Everyone is going to know I got dumped.

I look like a loser.

I AM a loser.

I feel humiliated.

I'm a failure.

They're gonna go off and start seeing other people, while I'm gonna be miserable and sad forever.

I'm horny ...and sad.

I'll never find anyone like them again.

They'll never find anyone like me again.... Right?

How could I have been so wrong / stupid / naive?

How can I trust anyone ever again?

How can I trust my own judgement ever again?

As anxious people, the thing that we desire most in our lives is control. If you're in control of a situation, or if you at least know what's going to happen, then you can plan ahead and prepare for it. When future events become unknown or uncertain, that's when our anxious instincts kick in and our brain starts to alert us that something's off. We have questions in our minds that are unanswered, so naturally we resort to making up answers for ourselves, even when they have no validity.

Here's something really important that I want you to understand:

The best way for you to take control of this situation is to acknowledge that

you have NONE

Yeah, you read that correctly. You have no power here, Gandalf the Grey. You have to relinquish all desire for control, because there's absolutely nothing you can do to force other peoples' behaviours and actions.

You can't stop people from talking. You can't stop your ex from telling their version of the story, whether it's the truth or not. You can't stop them from going out and living their life, or hooking up with the next wasteman/waste gyal they meet. You can't predict future events that haven't happened, and you'd be doing yourself a huge disservice stressing over something that's been totally fabricated in your mind with no solid evidence to support it.

Fully accepting that life is uncertain and unpredictable will grant you some peace of mind. Let go of any desire for control and just accept that so many things in this life are completely out of your control. This is how you give yourself peace and find solace. This is how you control the narrative: by focusing on the things that you *can* control.

In this moment, center your focus solely on what is within your control: *your body and your mind*. Those are the only things that truly matter at this point, so let's nurture and empower them as much as we can.

5 *THINGS TO GIVE YOURSELF*

1. Room to grieve

2. Space to cry

3. Time to heal

4. Permission to let go

5. Courage to move forward

Out of sight, out of mind . . .

Alright, before we go any further, there's one thing I need you to do.

You're not going to want to hear this. Every ounce of you is going to resist. But *trust me* when I say, **you need to do this.**

It's time to **unfollow your ex on all socials** *gasp*

NO ... OH, GOD, NO. NO, FUCK THAT ... ANYTHING BUT THAT! PLEASE! Yeah, yeah, I know. You're not ready. You can't. It's too soon. Blah, blah, blah. Listen ... there's only one reason you need to do this. And it's the only reason you need:

You two are broken up, and you're NOT getting back together

I'm not here to convince you that you and your ex aren't getting back together. Quite frankly, that decision should already have been made by one of you. If you're still stuck to the idea that you and your ex might get back together someday (even the slightest semi-reasonable possibility), then don't continue with this book. Write your own book and call it, *The Art of Toxic Relationships*.

At the end of the day, you're here because you have no intention to get back with them or keep them in your life. You want to move on. You're here because you can imagine a future version of yourself that's single, happy, and thriving. You won't be able to embrace the next chapter of your life if you're still clinging onto your ex, and onto an older version of yourself.

Therefore, there's absolutely no reason for you to be following them on social media and seeing what they're up to every day. Maybe you can be friends again someday—IF that's what you both want. But not right now. Right now, it's about distance, separation, and healing. Seeing them on social media is not going to contribute to any of that. It's only going to set you back 100,000 steps.

But wait ... there's more!

Not only are you going to unfollow them, but you're also going to **block** them so they can't see your shit either. I know it sounds excessive, but this is a necessary step. If you know they're viewing your socials, then you're always going to be conscious of it in the back of your mind, which will take you away from being present in whatever you're doing. Next thing you know, you're storying/posting a bunch of random stuff in the hopes that they're lurking in the shadows watching you. Newsflash: They're (probably) not. So just do you.

Take all the time you need...

SIKE

Do it now!

Take one final look and let them go, because you're not going to see their pages for a very long time, maybe ever again.

It sucks and I'm sorry (seriously—I know I'm being an asshole). There's resistance here because keeping them on your socials is a way to keep fragments of them in your life. It's probably the final thread connecting you to each other, and the feeling is almost like breaking up again. But look, you're not murdering them. You're not deleting their existence from the face of planet earth.

This is merely a step towards prioritizing your own well-being and healing. You have every right to protect your own heart and create the necessary space you need to move forward.

When it's done, you'll be proud of yourself for taking a huge step. And just remember: I'm your bestie, and I know what's best for you. So STFU and just do it, alright!?

Love you.

How are you feeling? Don't think. Just write.

ON GETTING BACK TOGETHER . . .

Let's talk about it . . .

Even having the slightest belief that you and your ex *might* get back together someday can hinder your healing process. To truly move forward, you first have to grant yourself permission to do so. This means accepting that the relationship is unequivocally over, rather than viewing it like it's a temporary break. This isn't a Ross and Rachel-type situation.

I know that's not easy to hear. It's hard to accept that it's over because, simply put, you wish it wasn't. You wish you could go back to the way it was. You wish that your ex was still present in your life and you could talk to them, and feel them, and carry on with the all the beautiful plans you had. You wish you could instantly make the pain go away, and getting back together is the simplest and quickest way to do that.

Is it *possible* that you and your ex could get back together someday?

Sure, exes get back together all the time. But that's only a band-aid solution. Both parties have to take the necessary time apart to grow and mature as single, independent people. That means wholeheartedly embracing the reality that your ex is no longer going to be part of your future. You broke up because the people that you both "were" at the time, wasn't the right combination. Whether within yourselves or your circumstances, something has to change.

For the time being, embrace this new chapter of your life. Once you've had some time to reflect and recover, you'll likely have a different perspective.

Heal, then see how you feel

Who are the three people you trust the most and can tell everything to?

#1: _____

RELATIONSHIP TO YOU: _____

#2: _____

RELATIONSHIP TO YOU: _____

#3: _____

RELATIONSHIP TO YOU: _____

Cool! These three people are your official **Meltdown Emergency Contacts (MECs).** You'll reach out to them whenever:

1) You're feeling sad, lonely, shitty, anxious, depressed, etc.

2) You're sober, drunk, high, and tempted to contact your ex at an ungodly hour. (don't you fucking dare).

3) You need to vent or just blow off some steam.

Be open and honest with your MECs. They're your MECs for a reason. Ask them to be patient with you and to support you throughout this journey. Most importantly, make sure they're people you know you can rely on and who will be there for you through thick and thin. Their presence and support is going to be crucial as you navigate the challenges ahead.

Managing expectations with friends...

Speaking of people being there for you, let's quickly chat about that.

I burned a lot of bridges after my last breakup. I did this weird thing where I kept tabs on people. I took mental notes of who was there for me at my low points, who reached out, who checked up on me, who made an effort to help me through everything ... and who didn't. I resented every single person who wasn't there. Every person who didn't call, didn't send me a text or a DM to see how I was holding up. Every person who I thought I could count on but ended up disappointing me.

Don't be like me

Remember when I said, "No one will truly know or understand what you're going through"? That especially applies to your friends and family. They aren't with you every minute of every hour of every day. So it would be unfair to put those kinds of expectations on them.

Maybe they just want to give you your space because they themselves are the type of people who like space after a breakup. Maybe they think you're absolutely crushing it and loving your new hot girl/boy era. Who knows? All they can see is what's on the surface. You're only going to torture yourself by stacking all your friendships up against each other as if everyone owes you something.

Also remember that everyone is going through their own shit. Just like you're focused on your healing journey, other people are striving for their own peace and happiness, too. They're not thinking about you, just like you're not thinking about them. So don't knock them for that.

Sometimes when we go through heartbreak, everything suddenly becomes about us (or at least that's what we think). Our world comes crashing down on us and we move as if it's happening to everyone else too. This hyper-focus on ourselves and our struggles can cause us to overlook our responsibilities and obligations towards others. We forget to check in on the people who matter most.

Reminder: Yes, you're heartbroken, AND you're still a friend, daughter/son, cousin, mentor/mentee, confidante, voice of reason, and so much more. You have relationships that you're still equally responsible for nurturing.

So, just as your friends will be there for you when you need them, make sure you're there for them too. Reach out, ask them how they're doing. Better yet, suggest meeting up to hang. As much as we love talking about ourselves, listening is a great way to gain perspective. There's also something really therapeutic about offering a shoulder for someone to lean on and knowing that we're all struggling together. That's what life is all about.

Here's an example of how NOT to treat a good friend through text:

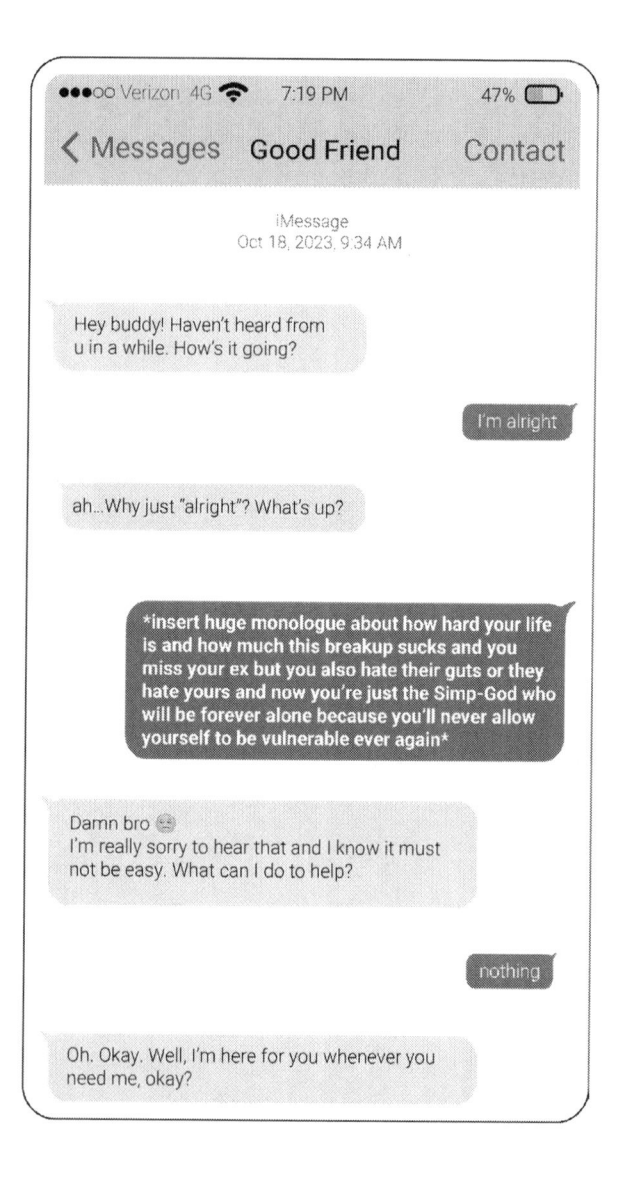

> **Good Friend:** Hey buddy! Haven't heard from u in a while. How's it going?
>
> **Me:** I'm alright
>
> **Good Friend:** ah...Why just "alright"? What's up?
>
> **Me:** *insert huge monologue about how hard your life is and how much this breakup sucks and you miss your ex but you also hate their guts or they hate yours and now you're just the Simp-God who will be forever alone because you'll never allow yourself to be vulnerable ever again*
>
> **Good Friend:** Damn bro 😒
> I'm really sorry to hear that and I know it must not be easy. What can I do to help?
>
> **Me:** nothing
>
> **Good Friend:** Oh. Okay. Well, I'm here for you whenever you need me, okay?

●●●○○ Verizon 4G 3:03 AM 11%

‹ Messages **Good Friend** Contact

Oct 23, 2023, 10:18 AM

Hey!
How you holding up, buddy?

Oct 25, 2023, 9:56 PM

Good

There you are!
Want to grab some dinner tomorrow?

Nah I'm good

Aw okay.
Well let me know when you're free. I want to make sure you're okay.

Oct 28, 2023, 1:03 AM

insert another giant monologue being petty and venting about your ex

provides sound and comforting words of encouragement, mixed with perfect balance of empathy and fresh perspective

leaves friend on read

Morale of the story:
DON'T BE AN ASS

On self-reflection...

The early stages of a breakup can be really difficult because it's a time when we start doing a shitload of self-reflection. We're stepping into an entirely unexpected chapter of our lives, one that we never asked for. Naturally, this transition period is going to prompt us to reflect on how and why the fuck we ended up here. We dig deep into ourselves and question not only *who* we are, but *where* we are at this stage of our lives. It's a little bit of an identity crisis. And trust me, the older you get, the harder you are on yourself.

Especially after getting your heart broken, it's really easy to pinpoint all the things that YOU think suck about your life and maybe even blame those things for why your relationship didn't succeed. Things like:

- Not making enough money.
- Or not being interesting enough.
- Or being insecure about your body
- Or still living at home with your parents.

(*thank you, social media, for making me feel like a piece of shit.)

It can be really difficult to try to navigate through all this when you're already at a very low point emotionally.

So here are a few daily reminders:

1) *A failed relationship doesn't mean that YOU failed as a person.* Regardless of who initiated the breakup, it doesn't mean that you weren't enough. It just means that you and your ex weren't compatible enough to make it through the incompatibilities. It also means that there's someone out there who complements you better. Someone who effortlessly ticks all the boxes and gives you everything you need to make you feel whole.

Imagine you were let go from your current job... *knock on wood*. Would that automatically mean you're a complete tool bag who's going to be unemployed for the rest of your life? Of course not. Maybe you were let go because the company did an internal re-structuring and you didn't fit with its future goals. Maybe it wasn't a job that fulfilled you, and in response, you didn't put in a whole lot of effort. Maybe your boss was a dickhead. Maybe you didn't see an actual future with the company, and you were just there because, well, what else were you gonna do? Maybe the job was sucking the life out of you, and you were already mentally checked out six months ago. Do you see where I'm going with this?

Just like jobs, there are a million reasons why relationships don't work out the way we expect. In some cases, we may have to take some responsibility. While in others, it may have been something completely beyond our control. Cut yourself some slack. If you take some time to reflect back on your relationship, you'll see that all the signs were there that this wasn't the right one for you.

2) In whatever ways you're not happy with your life (home, health, finances, etc.), *right now is the perfect time to set personal goals for yourself and chase after them.* You have the time, space, and freedom to do whatever you want to do. So why not now? What the fuck else do you have going on that's more important than your own happiness?

If you're going to be doing a bunch of self-reflection, why not also reflect on how far you've come? You're a completely different person than you were just six months ago. There were people in your life back then who are no longer part of your life now, and you're better for it. You're letting go of relationships that don't nourish your soul and creating space for healthier and more meaningful connections to blossom in your life.

You're learning to give fewer fucks about what other people think, you know why? Because you've realized that no one is thinking about you more than you are. Everyone is thinking about themselves. You're continuing to discover your personal boundaries and values and staying truer to them, even if it means parting ways with certain people. Every day, you're adding to your database of knowledge and experience. And every single thing that happens to you in your life, good or bad, is adding to that database.

Why not reflect on all the possibilities of where you can go from here? Right now, you're the only person standing in your way. And like I said from the start, no one is going to rescue you. No one is going to get you that promotion, or lift those weights for you , or push you across the finish line. Just like no one is going to write this damn book for me.

You have to will yourself to just fucking *do it*, even when you don't want to. You hold the reins of your destiny. You're smart, you care for your well-being, and you clearly have a vision for greatness in your future. You can do this. Getting up and walking out the door is literally the hardest part.

3) *Being miserable is a mindset.* Now let me clarify before you go screaming "TOXIC MASCULINITY." Yes, it's understandable to feel sad and discouraged because of everything that's going on. But it is 100% your choice whether or not you want to remain that way. Are you going to take action and allow yourself to move on from this breakup? If so, then the first step is to change your mindset so you can manifest positivity and encourage yourself to move forward.

Here's an example: You can probably come up with a list of 100 reasons why your life sucks ass. Or, you can just as easily come up with 100 reasons why your life is truly remarkable. Fight with that piece of shit inside your head as much as possible to do the latter. Listen to your Inner Cheerleader, not your Inner Hater. You're either going to destroy this breakup, or this breakup is going to destroy you. The choice is yours.

On gratitude . . .

Believe it or not, right now you have all the tools you need to start shifting your mindset to a place of peace and optimism. If you want to be happy, first you have to *choose* to be happy, then *allow* yourself to be happy. And it all starts with gratitude.

As cliché and oversimplified as it sounds, you have to focus on the good (I know, I'm a GENIUS, right?). Listen, it's as simple as showing appreciation for the little things that we take for granted every day.

Do you "have to" wake up for work tomorrow? No—you "get to" wake up for work tomorrow. You're blessed to have a job, a source of income that provides food on your plate and a roof over your head. Imagine you were going through everything you're currently going through, but on top of that, you were also unemployed and broke as fuck (OK, technically I have a job and I'm still broke as fuck, but you get the point). If you're still in school, that's a major blessing too. You have the opportunity to pursue a higher education (not everyone has this opportunity), and you're building the foundation for your future success.

Do you "only" have two friends? Nah—you have two amazing friends who love and respect you and want nothing but the best for you. Do you know how rare that is in today's day and age? These days, genuinely good and supportive friends are hard to come by. Yet, somehow, through the sea of fake-ass bitches, you were lucky enough to find two amazing humans who stick by your side through thick and thin. That's beautiful! Give me two loyal friends any day over a hundred fake ones. Period.

Are you single and "alone"? HELL NAH—you're single, BITCH! And you get to wake up tomorrow and do whatever the fuck you want. There's an entire world out there waiting for you. So seize the god damn day; it's an open canvas waiting for you to paint a masterpiece with experiences and memories.

Gratitude doesn't always come naturally to us. It takes practice and continuous effort. Any time you have a stream of negative thoughts enter your consciousness, tell that side of you to shut the fuck up immediately. Then get up and go sit at the cool kids' table.

Once you get the hang of it, you'll start noticing the difference in your life almost immediately.

Throughout this book, I will constantly be reminding you to show gratitude and write down your reasons to smile and tell the universe, "You're MY BITCH today." My hope is that you'll start doing this on your own, daily, with or without pen and paper. Notice how it changes your mood, your vibe, and uplifts your approach to each day.

Day of Gratitude

Write down five things you're grateful for today. They don't have to be big. Even a toasty warm cup of coffee in the morning is worth celebrating. If you get a good gratitude flow going and want to add more than five, go for it!

#1: _____

#2: _____

#3: _____

#4: _____

#5: _____

Check all that apply:

- [ ] Fuck my life; someone please punch me in the face so I feel something else besides the pain from this breakup.
- [ ] I cried more than ten times today.
- [ ] I'm single, bitch; let's fucking go!
- [ ] I'm still breathing ... unfortunately.
- [ ] I'm actually looking forward to seeing what today brings.
- [ ] I should probably get up and take a shower (it's been three days since I left my room).
- [ ] I wonder what my ex is doing. I'm gonna check their Insta-SIKE! What the actual fuck am I doing?
- [ ] I checked my ex's IG today using one of my burner accounts 'cause I'm a SIMPleton, and now I feel like absolute trash.
- [ ] I went outside today for the first time in a week.
- [ ] I didn't think about my ex the moment I opened my eyes this morning. Hallelujah!
- [ ] I masturbated then cried myself to sleep last night. Slept like a baby.
- [ ] I just want to be in a place where I don't need anyone else to fulfill my life.
- [ ] I'm never falling in love again. EVER. FUCK THAT.
- [ ] I would like to chug a 26er of vodka right now, please and thank you.
- [ ] I miss cuddles.
- [ ] Jesus, dating apps SUCK.
- [ ] Shit, I don't have *any* good pics for my Hinge profile.
- [ ] Please, Lord, don't let me see my ex on one of these apps. Only I'm allowed to move on.
- [ ] I'm so grateful for my friends.
- [ ] I wish I had more single friends to go out with.
- [ ] Thank God it's finally the weekend.
- [ ] Fuck my life, it's Monday.
- [ ] You know what? I dodged a bullet.
- [ ] Oh great, Valentine's Day is coming up.
- [ ] I'm sad but I know this is just temporary and I deserve so much more.
- [ ] Everything happens for a reason. This is just a small bump in the road.

A very harsh reality is that we're not always going to get the opportunity to say *everything* we want to say to our ex before the end; to leave it all out there with no regrets. And if and when the opportunity does present itself, we don't always communicate it in the best way.

It's only after the dust has settled that we're able to find clarity, formulate our thoughts, and piece everything together. But by that time, it's usually too late; communication has been lost, and/or at least one of you has emotionally checked out.

I know it's frustrating. It doesn't feel fair. You probably thought of so many valid and important points you should have gotten off your chest after the last conversation. It's annoying, but it's also not your fault. This isn't a trial where you have time to prepare your opening and closing statements. You needed time to process, and the time you needed wasn't given to you.

So now it's up to you to make that time for yourself. Let's pretend your ex is standing in front of you. Finish the sentences below:

I WISH _____

I WISH _____

I FEEL _____

I FEEL _____

I KNOW _____

I KNOW _____

I AM _____

I AM _____

Take a deep breath.

Inhale through the nose.

Exhale through the mouth.

YOU'VE SAID YOUR PIECE.

NOW GIVE YOURSELF PEACE.

DRAW HOW YOU FEEL

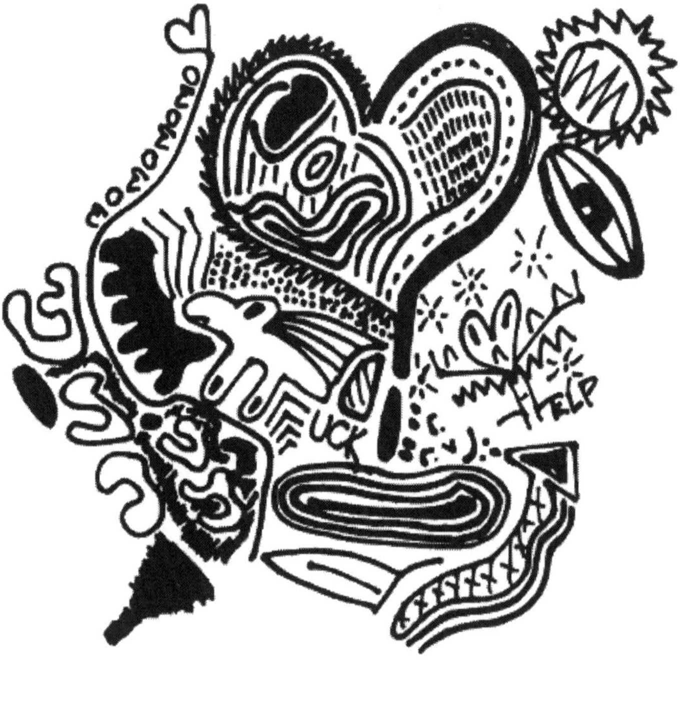
UCK
HELP

ON REBOUNDS . . .

I know it's going to be tempting. In fact, it might be one of the few things you're kinda looking forward to now that you're single.

Look, I'm not here to stop you, and I'm definitely not one to judge.

But here's the thing: **only do it if you know you're ready** and are willing to accept whatever feelings and consequences may follow. Some common side effects of premature rebounds include (but are not limited to):

- loneliness
- emptiness
- sin and regret
- deep-rooted shame
- feeling like an absolute piece of shit
- missing your ex so bad it physically hurts
- wanting to cuddle after but then realizing they're NOT your ex, and you get super uncomfortable and anxious so you end up going home at 4 a.m. but at least now you're in the comfort of your home where you can release the massive fart you've been holding in for the past three hours
- reminiscing on the past but only the good times
- crying yourself to sleep and waking up with the puffiest eyes that make you look like you just got jumped by a mob of allergies.

If you're not emotionally ready, there's a good chance you'll regret a rebound-type situation. Take it from me, **post-nut clarity** is a real thing, and it happens to both men and women. "Horny you" is the devil controlling you through your dick. Lil Wayne said it best, "It's like soon as I come, I come to my senses."

Take those horny goggles off. There is no worse feeling in the world than being heartbroken and alone after a regretful rebound. Don't put yourself (or the other person) in a situation that could potentially set you back when you're doing so well.

Trust me. Just jerk off before you make any rash decisions (this method has been proven to save lives).

THE
HURTING

Still here, insecure, white lines, warm beer,
Same bed, empty space, 1 mirror, 2-face,

New crib, not a home, blank screen, cell phone,
No calls, no texts, no love, just sex,

No sleep, black out, knock out, glass mouth,
Sober...sunup, relapse...sundown,

Used those air miles, switched up hairstyle,
Proclamation, declaration, Miley Cyrus, medication,

Christian, fiction, contradiction,
Heartbreak, cast out, crucifixion,

But I'll still make it out,
Like a maze, to a mouse,
GPS re-route,
Pray I don't bleed it out,

Checkpoint . . .

CONGRATULATIONS!

WELCOME TO THE HURTING!

So, at this point it's really started to sink in, and you're probably feeling like shit.

If you're hurting bad, *that's OK*. We're not going to try to make that pain go away (that's impossible anyways).

Instead, we have to acknowledge it, be present in it, and find ways to navigate through it, one day at a time.

On crying...

Sometimes it just feels good to cry (I googled it and something about the release of oxytocin and endogenous opioids which are basically endorphins. So, yeah, Science says so).

DON'T BE EMBARRASSED

Crying is a huge part of this process and can actually be beneficial to your healing when done in moderation—key word "moderation.."

There are rules when it comes to crying which you must swear to obey at all costs under penalty of being a big goofy Simp. Ladies and gentlemen, I present to you:

THE 10 CRY COMMANDMENTS:

RULE #1: THOU SHALT NOT CRY IN PUBLIC
Seems kind of obvious, but you'd be surprised how hard this one is. Let's say you're out at a party or social event and you're about to cry because a sudden wave of sadness comes over you. Your sensitive ass better leave that room immediately and pull your shit together. If you're not able to collect yourself and you're on the verge of breaking down, just leave the party and get your ass home, cause you're not gonna be THAT person at the function who's crying over their ex while everyone's trying to vibe and have a good time. Sorry, but this party ain't about you. Take it from me, because I've been that guy, and ten years later, I still CRINGE every time I think about it.

RULE #2: THOU SHALT NOT EVEN MENTION THE BREAKUP WHEN OUT IN PUBLIC
This is not something you share with anyone except your close circle. Be present in the moment. Enjoy your life. Have fun. Allow yourself to take in a

few hours of non-breakup energy. You can be sad again when you get home.

RULE #3: THOU SHALT NOT CRY IN FRONT OF CO-WORKERS, ACQUAINTANCES, AND DEFINITELY NOT STRANGERS

You're just gonna make people really uncomfortable. And then you'll have another thing to feel stupid and anxious about.

And if you must cry, you will obey the following parameter(s):

RULE #4: ONLY CRY IN PRIVATE OR IN FRONT OF YOUR MECs FROM PAGE 35

They're there to support you. Use them.

RULE #5: CRY AS HARD AS YOU NEED TO AND GET IT ALL OUT OF YOUR SYSTEM

This doesn't mean cry for hours and sulk in your misery all day every day. You get a pass for the first couple of weeks. But after that, fuck it. Pull yourself together because we've got bigger plans for you.

RULE #6: STAY HYDRATED

Water.

RULE #7: DON'T FILM YOURSELF CRYING AND POST IT ON TIKTOK

RULE #8: NEVER ... AND I MEAN ... EVERRRRR, CRY IN FRONT OF YOUR EX (AGAIN)

Holy shit, I cannot stress this one enough. You are not going to give your ex the satisfaction of watching you cry over them ... AGAIN. Hell-fuckin'-NO.

As Abel Tesfaye (a.k.a. The Weeknd) once said, *save your goddamn tears for another day.*

RULE #9:

Now that you know how hard it is, show compassion when you see others going through it.

RULE #10: BE KIND TO YOURSELF.

I know it's tough. In these moments, all you want is for the pain to go away because it's just so fucking hard to keep going. You're in the thick of the storm right now, but just remember that the storm will pass. You're stronger than you think, and you're moving closer to a beautiful horizon. Hang in there and be proud of yourself for how far you've come.

Write down 10 things you miss about your ex:

#1: I MISS _____

#2: I MISS _____

#3: I MISS _____

#4: I MISS _____

#5: I MISS _____

#6: I MISS _____

#7: I MISS _____

#8: I MISS _____

#9: I MISS _____

#10: I MISS _____

ON MISSING YOUR EX . . .

Sorry if that last page made you feel like shit. It's not something I want you to dwell on. But it is something I want you to acknowledge. Because it's OK to miss your ex. In fact, it would be kinda weird if you didn't.

For a long time, you saw, spoke to, and texted your ex every single day. You shared practically every aspect of your lives. Then all of a sudden, *poof*, in an instant, all of that is gone, and your mind has to shift from "we" to "me." You're no longer grocery shopping for two, cooking dinner for two, or making weekend plans for two. Anything to do with the future now has to be thought about in a completely different way, and this sudden change can leave a massive void in your life.

But a lot of times when we miss our ex, it's not actually the *person* that we miss. It's elements of what that person provided us throughout the relationship: companionship, intimacy, comfort, laughter, acceptance, sex, shnuggles.

In reality, you can get all of those things from other people and relationships in your life, like friends and family (minus the sex ... *awkward*). This is the perfect opportunity for you to grow your existing relationships and also build new ones.

Remember that everything you need to live a happy and fulfilling life is already right in front of you, inside of you, and all around you. The single life is not a life devoid of connection and satisfaction. You have an abundance of relationships in your life that will fill you with genuine love and positive energy. The most satisfying part is that your main source of fulfillment will now come from within you, first and foremost. It's not dependent on anyone else. It's something that you'll manifest and create from scratch. And everyone knows that "from scratch" is always more delicious.

Freehand write. Anything. Don't think. Just write:

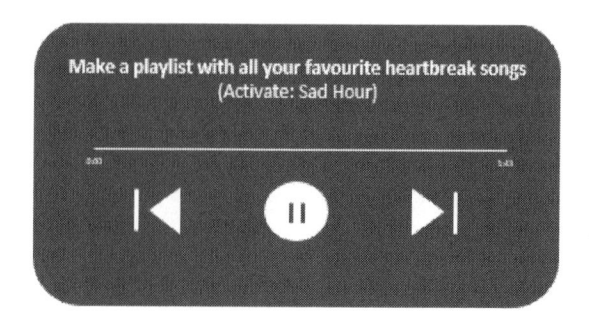

> **Make a playlist with all your favourite heartbreak songs**
> (Activate: Sad Hour)

I still have my playlist, and I listen to it all the time (not because I'm sad, but because I genuinely love the songs on there).

Music is truly an amazing form of breakup therapy and is going to help you a lot throughout this journey. People may not always be there, but music will. When you find that song or artist that perfectly encapsulates all of your emotions, you feel seen and supported. Sometimes that's all you really want in these moments: to know that you're not alone and that others are going through the same struggle.

Right now, these songs may be a painful reminder of a dark chapter in your life. But someday when this is all over, you'll listen to these songs again, and instead they'll be a reminder of how far you've come.

Check out my heartbreak playlist on Spotify

SEARCH: SOJU_KNOWS

PLAYLIST: BREAKING SAD

Tough pills to swallow...

1) If you truly want to move on, you need to let go of the idea that you and your ex *could* end up getting back together. It's not going to happen, and that's what you should be telling yourself.

2) Right person, wrong time, is still the wrong person.

3) Your ex owes you nothing. You owe them nothing. Live your life, and whatever they choose to do with theirs in none of your business.

4) Just like you, your ex is eventually going to move on. Yes, it hurts, but a little bit of time and self-care will get you through it. Refer back to #3.

5) If they really wanted to, they would have. Silence is the loudest answer they can give.

6) No one is going to rescue you from this breakup. The world is going to keep moving, with or without you. Stop feeling sorry for yourself. "Get your fucking ass up, and work."—The great American philosopher, Kim Kardashian.

7) Healing takes time—take a deep breath and keep yourself busy.

8) Ego is not your amigo.

9) If you're seeking revenge, you'll never get it, nor will it ever give you the satisfaction you think it will. Let that shit go.

10) You're not "starting all over." You're continuing a life-long journey of growth, and this is just one of many hurdles you'll go through.

11) You'll never be able to escape yourself or your pain through

drugs, alcohol, gambling, being a hoe, or other unhealthy habits. In order to heal, you need to confront and process all of your emotions with 100% clarity (a.k.a. sober).

12) No one is thinking about you more than you are thinking about you.

13) It's not the end, it's the beginning. Heartbreak is a pivotal moment in your life that represents the start of something new. The best is yet to come.

14) There's a difference between a relationship that was hard vs. one that was straight up painful.

15) Regret is the most destructive force in the universe.

16) Reflect on where you made mistakes and learn from them.

ON TAKING A DEEP BREATH (OR TWO)

I've only experienced one *real* panic attack in my life. It was a few months before the pandemic, less than 12 hours after my breakup, and 30 minutes before an important Zoom interview for a job that I *desperately* needed. I was in a terrible headspace that morning from the breakup the night before, so I went outside to my balcony to have a cigarette (I was smoking like a chimney during this period of my life). I came back inside and felt fine, but I noticed I was a little bit short of breath. Not uncommon for someone who just inhaled a thousand cancerous toxins into his lungs, I thought.

As I stared at my screen, suddenly my breathing got heavier. I felt dizzy and lightheaded. My heart rate picked up. I started having difficulty breathing and gasping for air. My heart was now beating out of my chest. Everything became a blur. I felt claustrophobic. The walls started closing in around me. I ran over to my bed in a panic. *I'm suffocating. I think I'm gonna faint. Oh, God, I'm dying. I'm gonna die! Fuck. Fuck. Fuck. Help me, God ... *yack*.* I vomited all over the floor and started crying hysterically, wailing like a madman.

30 minutes later—I join the Zoom call
Me: "Good morning! Nice to meet you."

I can't tell you how many times the simple act of mindful *breathing* has saved me while I was going through difficult periods in my life. Unfortunately for me, the above incident was NOT one of them. I'm not saying that breathing would have prevented me from having that panic attack (it was long overdue, TBH), but it definitely would have helped immediately after and probably would have improved my performance that interview. Oh, by the way, I didn't get the job—not even close.

If you're like me, this breakup has been causing you a lot of anxiety and overall uneasiness. There are so many thoughts and emotions to even attempt to sort through, all while feeling completely broken from the inside. It's overwhelming.

Throughout the rest of this book, I'm going to share with you some breathing exercises you can use whenever you feel anxious. I've made it a common practice in my life to meditate and *breathe* daily throughout the day: morning, afternoon, right before bed, even in the middle of the night if I can't fall back asleep. Try them out and do what works best for you. Each session should only take about 2-5 minutes, so no excuses. I promise it will make a huge difference.

Keep calm and breathe on.

BREATHING EXERCISE

1. Get comfortable.

2. Close your eyes and place your hands on your stomach.

3. Breathe in and out slowly and **count to 50** with each breath. In through the nose, out through the mouth.

4. Focus on the breath as it enters and leaves your body. Feel your hands on your stomach as it expands and compresses with each breath.

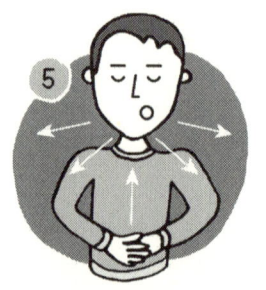

5. Nose inhale ... 1
Mouth exhale ... 2
Nose inhale ... 3
Mouth exhale ... 4

6. Count all the way to 50. Be present in this moment. Don't think about **ANYTHING** but breathing. Nice and slow.

A reminder that throughout this journey, you're going to have *some* setbacks (or a lot). They'll come in many forms: calling/texting your ex and getting left on read, getting blackout drunk/high to numb yourself, a rebound that makes you feel 100 times worse, a complete mental breakdown, or even just feeling like you're never going to move on from this.

These setbacks are all part of the journey. Stop being so hard on yourself. Recalibrate, take a deep breath, then another one—then get back up and keep going.

*D*AY OF GRATITUDE

Write down five things you're grateful for today:

#1: _____

#2: _____

#3: _____

#4: _____

#5: _____

Losing someone important is like losing part of your identity.

After a breakup, it's not just one person you end up losing. You lose the entire social circle you both hung out with on a regular basis. You lose connection with so many people that you got close with because of your ex. You can't go to the same places you both used to go. You can't do the same kinds of activities. All this change happens at once, and it sucks.

This new life and identity make you stop feeling like yourself, like you don't even know who you are anymore. You're no longer living in the present. You're just a zombie trying to get through the day. This might lead you to do things out of character, to act in ways you'd never want your mother to see. For me, I did a LOT of drugs. It was my way of escaping; an easy way to feel artificially good for a short moment. The aftereffect was that I became more depressed and lashed out on everyone over the most minor things.

I read somewhere that during a breakup, there's a constant yearning to *escape yourself*. You no longer want to be the old you. The old you got you into this mess. So, you fill your life with distractions, people, and choices that take you away from the essence of who you are. Next thing you know, you're looking in the mirror and don't even recognize the person staring back at you.

It's scary to suddenly be forced to navigate through the world on your own, isn't it? Your ex was such a *huge* part of your life. It's been so long since you had to do things independently and to think from a completely solo mindset; it's terrifying.

But always remember: *You had an entire life before they showed up.*

You were someone before you met them, and you will continue to be someone after them. The show must go on. The show *will* go on.

Change is good; embrace it. Try new things and don't be afraid to step out of your comfort zone, as long as you stay true to your core values.

Make it a habit to check in with yourself each day and ask, "Am I leading a life that's nurturing my mind, body, and soul?"

A daily reminder to:

STOP GLORIFYING YOUR EX
STOP PUTTING THEM ON A PEDESTAL

#1
Your ex was NOT perfect.

#2
Your relationship was FAR FROM perfect.

#3
There's a reason why things DIDN'T WORK OUT.

Write down 10 things that were WRONG about your ex and/or the relationship:

#1: _____

#2: _____

#3: _____

#4: _____

#5: _____

#6: _____

#7: _____

#8: _____

#9: _____

#10: _____

Take a picture of this page and keep it on your phone. Fuck it, make it the damn Lock Screen. Read it every time you miss your ex. It helps.

WHAT'S YOUR MANTRA FOR THIS BREAKUP?:

mantra
/ (ˈmæntrə, ˈmʌn-) /

noun
any sacred word, phrase, or syllable used as an object of concentration and embodying some aspect of spiritual power.

That's right, your mantra is gonna give you some *spiritual powers*. Here are some ones that I like:

> *"Remember that sometimes not getting what you want is a wonderful stroke of luck."*
> **—Dalai Lama**

> *"Letting go means to come to the realization that some people are a part of your history but not a part of your destiny."*
> **—Steve Maraboli**

> *"Pain is inevitable, Suffering is optional."*
> **—Haruki Murakami**

In essence, mantras are the most fire rap bars, but heartbreak edition

If you don't have a mantra, find one! Google "breakup quotes" or "motivational quotes." Song lyrics are great too. Be selective and take time to find one that really resonates. Write it in the space below (please don't get it tattooed):

You loved your ex a lot. And guess what? They loved you too (at least for a time, and in their own way).

But remember that *love alone is never enough to make a relationship work*. The little things matter: trust, communication, respect, honesty, vulnerability, having similar life goals, compatible lifestyles, being on the same page (OK, these are all big things).

But even the little things: liking enough of the same movies/shows/music/food/activities, daily routines, being able to fit into each other's emotional rhythms, doing small gestures and acts of service for each other, being able to say sorry and "I love you." You can have all the love in the world for each other, but if you're not on the same vibe, those differences will quickly reveal themselves.

My old man used to say, "Find someone who's singing the same song." And that always stuck with me.

Think about your last relationship. Something was off about it that had you both out of sync. Your energies may have matched initially during the honeymoon phase and the good times, but more importantly, did they match during the bad times?

Was your ex impossible to reason with during arguments?
Were they so stuck in their own head that they couldn't see things from any angle other than their own?
Were they toxic and hurtful when they were upset?
Was there something about you that they couldn't get on board with (or vice versa)?

There are so many reasons why our energies and personalities don't always mesh. But that's never an excuse for disrespectful behaviour or actions that cross your boundaries.

Love yourself enough to accept that you deserve someone who's singing the same song; someone who gives and receives the same energy as you. Your ex was not the one.

BREATHING EXERCISE

1. Get comfortable. Relax your neck and shoulders.

2. Inhale slowly through your nose for **two Mississippis.**

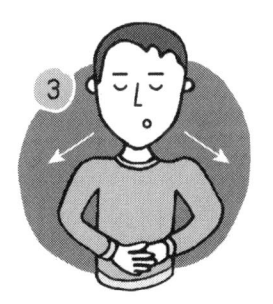

3. Pucker your lips and **whistle** (softly) as you slowly exhale for **four Mississippis.**

4. Close your eyes and repeat for 2 minutes.

Tell me why your day was ass.

"You can miss someone every day and still be glad that they're no longer in your life."

—**Oprah**
via a random TikTok

(What? You try coming up with 200 pages of original content)

If the relationship was the only thing that defined *you*, you weren't ready to be in one to begin with.

Rebuilding yourself doesn't mean solely focusing on you. It means nurturing the abundance of relationships in your life that give you purpose.

Focus your energy towards sending kindness and positivity into the world.

Now is the perfect time to get a fresh start in as many aspects of your life as possible.

Is there something that you've been wanting to do for a while but just never had the time or motivation? Stop thinking. Put it into action.

It's *never* too late.

Stan Lee published his first comic book hit at age 39.
Vera Wang opened her first boutique at age 40.
Samuel L. Jackson landed his breakout role in *Pulp Fiction* at age 46.
Colonel Sanders started KFC at age 62.

Let's take a step back for a second. Would you *ever* want to be with someone who's still hung up on their ex? Someone who's just with you to try and fill a void from their last relationship? Someone who has one foot in, and one foot out?

Helllll nah—you want someone who's looking towards the future. Someone who's continuously working to be the best version of themselves and unlock their full potential. Someone who has their own thing going on, who values themselves and isn't going to just drop everything for the sake of being in a relationship. Someone who's patient and understands that anything worthwhile takes time.

The best relationships are the ones where two happy and independent people come together to co-exist as one.

Your job is to do your part and get to where you need to be spiritually, mentally, and physically. The only thing you can control is how you show up for yourself every single day. There is no excuse not to.

Showing up for YOU starts now.

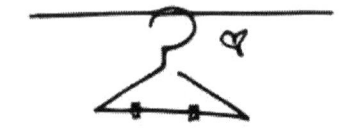

If you could have it your way, how would everything have turned out?

We don't always get the ending we want. But trust me, we *always* get the ending we need. We've all had relationships, including friendships, that we thought would last forever but abruptly came to an end. When you're going through it in the moment, it hurts. But as time goes on, you'll realize it was something that needed to happen.

In *Kung Fu Panda*, Master Oogway says to Shifu, "One often meets his destiny on the road he takes to avoid it." I know it doesn't feel like it right now, but one day you'll look back on this breakup and thank the fucking universe for crushing you into pieces. Because it was only through this that you were able to finally let go of what was never meant for you.

The best art in the universe is created through intense suffering.

Day of Gratitude

Write down five things you're grateful for today:

#1: _____

#2: _____

#3: _____

#4: _____

#5: _____

Tell me about the biggest fight you ever had with your ex:

Why was that one so bad?

Looking back now with 20-20 hindsight, what did that fight teach you?

The biggest fights revealed signs of fundamental differences between you and your ex, especially when they happened repeatedly. Keep reminding yourself of these differences. They were *clear signs of incompatibility* that would have come back to bite you in the ass down the road. Remember how they treated you in those moments. Remember how immaturely they acted when you spoke your truth. Be thankful that you got to peek behind the curtains and see their true selves.

Talk shit about your ex. Go off.

Cool.

NOW RIP THIS PAGE OUT
AND <u>THROW IT IN THE TRASH</u>

We aren't holding on to this kind of energy EVER. We're going to transform this into a positive and invest it back into YOU.

How are you holding up? Making some progress?

If you don't think you're making any progress, respectfully, you're wrong.

It might not feel like it, but you've been slowly healing a little bit every day since we started this journey together. Remember that wounds don't heal right away, nor in an instant. Have you noticed that you can never pinpoint the *exact* moment a papercut has fully healed? It just happens gradually. At some point after enough time has passed, you stop thinking about it. Next thing you know, you look down at your finger and the cut is fully healed.

You're going to heal from this breakup in the same way. There won't be a single moment of actualization. It'll just happen. Over time you'll start thinking about it less and be able to focus on other things that make you happy.

You'll go to the beach with your friends and lie in the sun and appreciate just how lucky you are to be living in that moment. You'll put on that beautiful fit that makes you feel like the Rizzard of Oz. You'll kill that presentation at work that you were so nervous about and spent all week preparing for. You'll spend time with your parents and realize how much you missed being around them and that you should do it more often while you still can. You'll go out for drinks with your co-workers and network and meet the person who's going to help you land that next role. You'll buy groceries and cook yourself a delicious meal and be fully at peace as you binge your favourite show in the comfort of your home. You'll get under the covers and just before you turn off the light, you'll think to yourself, "You know what? Today wasn't so bad."

That's how this healing thing works. You're on the right track.

Keep going... It gets better.

Tell me about the hardest thing you ever had
to deal with in your life (other than this):

What got you through it?

I just want to take this opportunity to tell you that you're doing amazing.

Take a deep breath

Drink water

Get some sunlight

Keep going.

I've never met you. But if you're here reading this, I think I know you a little bit.

You're the type of person who wears their heart on their sleeve. You're resilient. You're a ride or die. You don't give up on a relationship just because you've run into some tough times. Once you're committed to something, you do everything in your power to make it work.

You care... A LOT. You love even more. You follow your heart, even when every cell in your body tells you not to. And sometimes that ends up getting you hurt. Your friends and family often say to you, "I told you so," and yeah, they probably did a million times.

But guess what? They didn't have all the facts. Yes, they tried to warn you, and in hindsight, you probably should have taken their advice. But they weren't there to experience all those moments that kept you holding on.

Every single one of us has that friend who was in that god-awful relationship where we were like, **"Why the hell are you still with them?"** And we tried to tell them, but they wouldn't listen, right?

The Answer: Same reason you were. Because your friend fell in love with a side of them that no one else saw.

You fell in love and you went all in. You ended up getting hurt, but that's okay. Don't ever be ashamed for giving all of yourself to someone you believed in, for being vulnerable and trusting them with your whole heart. That's what you're supposed to do. You get to walk away from this thing knowing that you gave it everything you had and left it all on the table.

On anxious thoughts . . .

Anxious thoughts are normal; we all have them, and they come in all shapes and sizes. It's your mind preparing you for future events that may or may not ever happen. It's your way of convincing yourself, "I'm in control here because I've meticulously thought out every possible scenario." But anxious thoughts become crippling when we allow them to take over our very existence.

"They've probably moved on and are already hooking up with other people."

"What's everyone going to think about me after this?"

"They're doing just fine, and meanwhile I'm here looking like Simpy Simpington."

Ever heard the saying, "Don't cry over spilled milk" or "Water under the bridge"? Stop wasting your time and energy on things that are completely out of your control, especially things that have already happened and are now in the past.

Here's what we know:

One aspect of your life has come to an end. A hundred new ones are about to begin.

Not knowing where life is going to take you can be unsettling, but it can also be exciting and full of possibilities.

Yep, you're SINGLE

And you know what? It's OK that you're single. In fact, it's exactly what you need to be right now... until you're ready for your next relationship.

Your life is more than your romantic life. YOU are more than your romantic life.

Your anxious thoughts may have already happened, or maybe they didn't. Maybe they will happen, maybe they won't. Who the hell knows? The more unnecessary attention you give them, the deeper down the rabbit hole you'll go, and the more they'll fuck with your inner peace.

Do you want to be in a positive spiral or a negative spiral? It's up to you.

The best way to counter your anxious thoughts is to focus on the things you *can* control:

> Your healing
> Your growth
> Your happiness.

These are the only things that matter now, and all future decisions should be predicated on these three things only.

Heartbreak is a master manipulator.

Here's an exercise for you whenever you're having negative thoughts. Ask yourself these questions:

- Is there any real evidence to support my thoughts?
- Is there any evidence directly contradicting my thoughts?
- Am I interpreting this situation without all the evidence?
- What would my best friend (a.k.a Ben), say about this?

Here's a real-life example:

Negative thought:
My ex has probably moved on and is fucking other dudes and living her best life.

Is there any real evidence to support my thoughts?
Technically no. This is all speculation. I saw her in a mutual friend's IG story, and there was a dude's arm in the background, and he has tattoos (I don't know why that's relevant but it probably means they're fucking.)

Am I interpreting this situation without all the evidence?
100% yes. I know I'm trippin', but I can't help it. I'm just looking at everything from the most negative lens because, damn, that's all my life has been lately.

What would my best friend have to say about this?
They would tell me: "You idiot. It doesn't matter whether she is or isn't fucking someone else. It's no longer relevant to you and it's none of your business. Focus on yourself, continue your growth and healing journey, and live your best life because (apparently) that's what she's doing too. Don't you deserve the same? You say you're looking at everything with a negative lens because that's all your life has been? No, dummie. It's the opposite. Your life has been all negative because that how you've chosen to look at it.

I love this exercise and still use it to this day. It helps to calm me down and see my negative thoughts for what they really are: *me just straight up TRIPPIN'*.

Take a step back and look at the situation objectively and free of bias. You'll quickly see the flaws in your way of thinking.

How ya feeling today? Let's talk about it:

Your ass deserves a break.

Take a whole day to just relax and do something that makes you feel good.

Go for a run in nature, pick up your favourite meal, shower up, then binge a show. Treat yourself.

Seriously ... Call in *sick*, turn on your "out-of-office" and take an entire day free of responsibilities. Yeah, yeah. I know work is super busy right now. (When is it not?) I know you've got lots of shit you need to take care of. But don't worry. It'll all still be there waiting for you when you get back.

We need to normalize taking time to ourselves to prioritize our mental health. Bitch, we deserve it!

*D*AY OF GRATITUDE

Write down five things you're grateful for today:

#1: _____

#2: _____

#3: _____

#4: _____

#5: _____

ON FORGIVENESS . . .

Forgiveness is one of the most powerful tools we have when it comes to healing from a breakup. But it's also one of those things that's difficult as fuck to put into practice.

When someone wrongs us, it's hard to forgive because we know we have every right to be angry, and the person who wronged us doesn't deserve our forgiveness. On top of that, you want them to *own up to their fuckup.* "Why should I be the bigger person?"

But here's the thing: when you forgive, it doesn't mean you're giving that person a pass, or that you just have to "deal with it" and pretend nothing happened.

Instead, you're saying: "I'm letting go of any anger, resentment, shame, and any other negative feelings that you put on me today. And I'm no longer going to allow those feelings to affect me from this day forward."

So, in that respect, forgiveness is not something that you do for others. Forgiveness is something you do for yourself. You're giving yourself permission to move on and be happy. That's how you be the "bigger person."

I promise you, when you learn to forgive, your life will become exponentially more peaceful. It's one of the most liberating things you can do for yourself.

*I*T'S *TIME TO FORGIVE YOUR EX*

Dear

#1: I forgive you for

#2: I forgive you for

#3: I forgive you for

#4: I forgive you for

#5: I forgive you for

Now forgive yourself

Dear me,

#1: I forgive you for

#2: I forgive you for

#3: I forgive you for

#4: I forgive you for

#5: I forgive you for

BREATHING EXERCISE

1. Get comfortable.

2. Take your **right hand** and press your **thumb** against your **right nostril** to block the hole.

3. Inhale through your **left nostril** ...*hold it*... then close your **left nostril** with your **index finger.**

4. Release your **thumb** and exhale through your **right nostril.**

5. Inhale through your **right nostril**, and repeat.

6. The pattern should go like this:
*Left nostril inhale // Right nostril exhale
Right nostril inhale // Left nostril exhale
Left nostril inhale...*

Do this for two minutes.

ON AVOIDING YOUR EX . . .

If you're lucky, you dated someone outside of your friend group, and after the breakup you don't really have to worry about bumping into them again.

If you're not so lucky (like me), you dated someone from directly within your friend group, or neighborhood, or workplace (rookie mistake), and now your life is a pain in the ass because you have to see your ex everywhere you go, or their name gets brought up constantly.

Your initial reaction is probably going to be, "I need to avoid this person at all costs," so you opt to stay in rather than spending time with your friends. And yeah, that's all good and well because technically, you're doing the right thing by cutting off the possibility of contact with your ex.

But this becomes a problem when you stop enjoying your own life out of fear of running into your ex. You stop going to group hangouts, or you miss out on special celebrations and milestones with your friends, and you basically go MIA. You cut off all ties with the world so that you can stay in your little bubble where it's safe. So here's my advice to you:

Stop being a little BITCH

Just kidding. No, but seriously. You can't let one person stop you from living your life, especially your ex. Your friends and family deserve more from you. And you deserve more from your friends and family.

A broken heart is never an excuse to not show up for the people that matter.

I'm not saying it's not going to be awkward to be around your ex again, because it probably will be. But you'll get through it, and trust me, it won't be as bad as you're imagining it. When faced with situations like these (ones that you've been actively trying to avoid), these are the times when you grow the most and can quantify your growth. It's like an alcoholic who's been sober for the last six months. An incredible milestone is when they're finally able to go to an event where alcohol is present and not have a single drop or spiral.

What's most important is your commitment to your friends and family. You don't have to go to every event. Be selective about which social outings you need to attend and which ones you can sit out. And if you do see your ex, be polite. Say hello, keep it brief and move on.

Every day is a new day to work on yourself. Here are six ways:

#1:

Learn something new—
Sign up for a class or workshop that interests you.

#2:

Get in the best shape of your life. Revenge bod is never a bad thing.

#3:

Map out a 1-2 year plan to land that dream job and get after it.
Tunnel vision.

#4:

Read more. Everyday. All the time.

#5:

Start a side hustle and secure the bag. Because "laa, laa, la-la, wait til I get my money right." – Kanye West

#6:

Travel ... Travel some more ... And then travel some more again.
Never stop travelling. Did I mention travel?

Get your ass up and start living. Be who you were born to be, not who *they* wanted you to be.

DAY OF GRATITUDE

Write down five things you're grateful for today:

#1: _____

#2: _____

#3: _____

#4: _____

#5: _____

ON YOUR LIVING SPACE . . .

It's not just a place where you eat, poop, and sleep. It's where you LIVE. Your fortress, your *maison*, your home base, your sanctuary, your place of Zen.

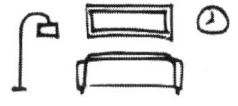

The environment in which you live has a ginormous impact on your mood, energy, and overall well-being. Your home is an embodiment and extension of you. So, if it looks like a complete shitshow and is full of dust and clutter, guess what? Your mind is going to be a direct reflection of that.

Little things like making your bed every single morning can have an enormous impact on your daily life. Just like your mind, your living space needs continuous care and maintenance. The longer you wait to take out the trash or do the dishes and allow the shit to pile on, the more a pain in the ass it'll be to clean up, and the less you'll want to do it.

Besides, no self-respecting adult should be living like they're in a frat house. I'm amazed how many grown-ass adults won't even take 10 minutes to tidy up before having guests over. HUGE red flag.

Imagine bringing a date home and you've got a sink full of dishes, dirty laundry everywhere, and skid marks all over your toilet. Bruh, no one needs to see that shit (literally), especially someone you're trying to impress.

Rule of thumb:

If it takes less than 2 minutes, do it now.

That includes taking out the trash, wiping the kitchen counter, throwing a load of laundry in the dryer, and of course, wiping those beautiful shit stains.

Be consistent. Respect your living space, take care of it on a regular basis, and make sure to give it a deep clean every 2-3 weeks. This will give you the physical and mental space to focus on the things that really matter: you and your healing journey.

A friendly reminder as you embark on this beautiful day:

YOU ARE LOVED

Write down five people who love you and *why* they love you.

#1: _____

_____

#2: _____

_____

#3: _____

_____

#4: _____

_____

#5: _____

_____

Some people desperately want a long-term relationship but aren't willing to go through the not-so-great days; the days when you argue four times in the same week; the days full of doubt and uncertainty; the days where a million stupid things are trying to tear you apart; the days when it feels like you're the only one keeping the relationship alive; the days when you can't suppress your jealous intrusive thoughts; the days when you're struggling financially; the days when it feels like you've lost your purpose and all you need is someone there to remind you of how wonderful you are.

Relationships aren't amazing all the time. Sometimes they suck. Sometimes we think it would be more convenient to *not* be in them. And that's all part of it. They require hard work, commitment, trust, communication, and resilience. Some people will hit a rough patch in their relationship and automatically jump into panic mode. They'll assume there's a serious flaw in the relationship, or worse, in you. These people don't understand the ebbs and flows of relationships.

Real relationships evolve in many ways over time, and they move in all different directions: forwards, backwards, up, down, even sideways. *What's most important is that both parties are committed to moving in all those directions together.*

Every once in a while, one person might have to carry more weight than the other, and that's OK. This all comes down to maturity. I previously talked about finding someone *who's singing the same song*, someone on the same frequency. Part of that means both of you have to be emotionally mature enough to stay the course and shut out any doubt during the inevitable "tough times." Doubt is one of the greatest cancers of relationships. A single seed of doubt can grow into insecurity, distrust, regret, disconnection, and a yearning for something else. That's when people start to pull away and explore other options.

Ask yourself: Was my ex emotionally mature enough to be in a committed partnership? Was I?

In my case, any time we argued more than once within the same week, a cloud of doubt would immediately hang over our heads. Suddenly, our whole relationship was in question. The fear of her breaking up with me at any moment was physically and mentally draining. I felt like I was constantly walking on eggshells, and the burden was on me to prove that our relationship was worth it—that *I* was worth it. It took a toll on me and ate away at my self-esteem. I started to believe that maybe she was right. I wasn't worth it. I was the problem. I became a shell of myself, constantly in fear that she would leave if I didn't live up to her expectations.

In the end I realized the answer to my question was: Hell Fucking No—she was not ready

A person who expects *everything* to be easy will never truly understand the value of anything. If love were something you could have with anyone and everyone, then what would make it special? The things in this world that have the most value are the things you have to work your ass off for.

Breakups make you realize that you can **LOVE** someone so fucking much . . . and . . . **HATE** their guts at the same damn time.

Day of Gratitude

Write down five things you're grateful for today:

#1: ⎯⎯⎯⎯⎯⎯⎯⎯⎯⎯⎯⎯⎯⎯⎯⎯⎯⎯⎯⎯⎯⎯⎯⎯⎯⎯⎯⎯⎯⎯⎯⎯⎯⎯⎯⎯⎯⎯⎯

#2: ⎯⎯⎯⎯⎯⎯⎯⎯⎯⎯⎯⎯⎯⎯⎯⎯⎯⎯⎯⎯⎯⎯⎯⎯⎯⎯⎯⎯⎯⎯⎯⎯⎯⎯⎯⎯⎯⎯⎯

#3: ⎯⎯⎯⎯⎯⎯⎯⎯⎯⎯⎯⎯⎯⎯⎯⎯⎯⎯⎯⎯⎯⎯⎯⎯⎯⎯⎯⎯⎯⎯⎯⎯⎯⎯⎯⎯⎯⎯⎯

#4: ⎯⎯⎯⎯⎯⎯⎯⎯⎯⎯⎯⎯⎯⎯⎯⎯⎯⎯⎯⎯⎯⎯⎯⎯⎯⎯⎯⎯⎯⎯⎯⎯⎯⎯⎯⎯⎯⎯⎯

#5: ⎯⎯⎯⎯⎯⎯⎯⎯⎯⎯⎯⎯⎯⎯⎯⎯⎯⎯⎯⎯⎯⎯⎯⎯⎯⎯⎯⎯⎯⎯⎯⎯⎯⎯⎯⎯⎯⎯⎯

On closure . . .

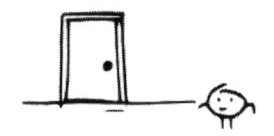

Why do we need closure? What is closure, anyways?

Let me paint you a little picture: You and your ex are sitting on the floor in a dimly lit room with 964 candles surrounding you, each one representing the exact number of magical days you spent together on this Earth. You engage in a divine ritual where you both read handwritten letters to each other out loud, and hug and cry it out, while "Godspeed" by Frank Ocean is playing in the background. This is the last moment you'll share together before you bid each other farewell. It's fucking beautiful.

Broken record sound effect

SIKE, obviously I'm joking because that's never how it goes, but you get the picture, right? This is an ideal scenario of how we want closure to go: We want a squeaky-clean breakup where we're able to tie up all the loose ends and say our goodbyes with respect and compassion. We want to fully understand why the relationship is ending *and* be at peace with whatever those reasons are. Most importantly, we want to feel "seen" and have our feelings and emotions acknowledged by the other person. In other words, we want the breakup to happen on *our terms* so that we can move on with our lives.

The problem is, this rarely happens. There's always something that doesn't go our way, whether it's a lack of communication, empathy, or a sense of abandonment and betrayal. This is a really shitty feeling because from our perspective, there are still things that haven't been fully acknowledged for the breakup to officially come to a close.

The unfortunate truth you'll have to accept at some point is that you may never get the "closure" you want and deserve. In most cases, you won't even get a final opportunity to speak to them in person with 100% clarity, to clearly communicate your side of the story, and ultimately understand: Why?

Why couldn't we just work out our differences and live happily ever after?

When this happens, closure needs to come from within *you*.

Accept that from this point forward, your ex's decisions and behaviours are out of your control.

Accept that you did everything you could to make the relationship work, or maybe you didn't. Either way, accept that you did what you did, and now it's over.

Accept the fact that your ex did not give you the closure you deserve, and that says *a lot* about them.

It's spilled milk. There's nothing you can do to change it. You deserve better, you're not going to settle for less, and that's all the closure you need.

BREATHING EXERCISE

1. Get comfortable.

2. Inhale through your nose for a **count of four**.

3. Exhale through your mouth for a **count of eight**.

Close your eyes and repeat for two minutes or more.

IMPORTANT - PLEASE READ

I cannot stress enough how important exercise is in your healing journey. Exercise does and will make you feel infinitely better.

Listen, I get it. When you're going through heartbreak and you're depressed AF, the last thing you want to do is go to the gym. Breakups are exhausting, and they drain all the life out of you. But these are the moments when the universe is really trying to test you.

You can choose to stay home, be sad, and sulk in your misery; or you can get up, dedicate everything you have to your well-being, and become the best damn version of yourself.

You are the main character in this story. You are the person who decides how this story ends. Take control of your narrative. Trust me; the hardest part is walking out the door.

How's it going today?

Day of Gratitude

Write down five things you're grateful for today:

#1: ....

#2: ....

#3: ....

#4: ....

#5: ....

Put your phone away today and just be present. Only look at it for emergency calls/texts.

NO SOCIAL MEDIA

Come back and check one of the boxes below at the end of the day:

- ☐ I did it! Piece of cake.
- ☐ Mostly fail... I'll try again tomorrow.
- ☐ Epic fail. I'm a piece of shit and **literallyyy** can't live without my phone (but I swear I'll try again tomorrow).

If you struggled with this challenge, take a second to think about how beneficial it would be to spend even one less hour a day on your phone. By the end of the week, that's seven whole hours where you could have put your energy towards something positive for yourself.

I know that being away from social media can leave you feeling isolated and disconnected. But trust me when I say this, you're not missing out on anything important, because the things/people that are most important will always find their way to you.

Don't get me wrong. I love social media, especially TikTok. For most of us, it's where we get 90% of our news about what's happening in the world. I'm not one of these oldheads who thinks all social media is rotting your brain, because that's simply not true.

But social media *is* like a drug, and like any drug with stimulating and addictive qualities, you need to self-assess your intake and manage it accordingly. You need to set boundaries for yourself and know when to take a break. You need to recognize when certain content is for you, and when it's not.

I deactivated my Instagram account over two years ago because that shit just didn't make me feel good. I would see people's posts and think, "Why not me?" I would try to impress people who I didn't even like. I would post stories of me out partying and check the "views" every two minutes, hoping I'd get noticed by people who gave 0 fucks about me. I would try to increase my follower count as if it were a direct indication of my relevance in the world (on some Black Mirror-type shit.) I would even post all my successes and accomplishments with the goal that my exes would see them and feel shitty about themselves. I did all of these things thinking they were proof that I mattered and that I was happy. But none of this shit matters. We post pictures, we get a bunch of likes and a cheap hit of dopamine. Then what?

The best thing you can do for yourself is take regular breaks from the world of social media and be present in the real world. DO YOU. Fully unplug and do cool things without having the need to share it online.

"Real Gs move in silence like Lasagna."

- Lil Wayne

True love will

ALWAYS

meet you halfway.

Day of Gratitude

Write down five things you're grateful for today:

#1:

#2:

#3:

#4:

#5:

On drugs and alcohol . . .

Remember in 6th grade when they first told you about drugs and alcohol, and how they'll destroy your life if you go anywhere near them?

Well kids, this is the ONE time where I kind of agree.

Drugs and alcohol do not mix with heartbreak. This is a fact. They'll give you temporary relief to numb the pain, but life will inevitably force you to face the music.

I know I've been ramming this into your brain throughout this journey; it's so important during these times to be at your best both physically and mentally. At the peak of my breakup, I was going on all-night benders until 6 in the morning at least 2-3 times per week. I'd sleep all day, eat instant ramen or fast food in the afternoon, and go back to sleep until it was dark again. I repeated this cycle for six months straight. Just imagine the mental and physical toll it took on me. Physically, I lost 15 pounds. My face looked like a cross between a zombie and a skeleton. My skin was dry and scaly, and my lips barely had any colour. I had no energy or desire to do anything other than get absolutely fucked out of my mind. Mentally, I was severely depressed, anxious, and irritable. I got triggered by the most trivial things. It quickly became a vicious cycle, and I was starting to lose myself and let down the people closest to me. I knew that if I didn't make a change soon, I'd probably end up dead (which actually sounded very appealing at the time).

I realized that if I wanted to get over this breakup and turn my life around, I had to completely remove drugs and alcohol from the equation. I had to free myself from those temptations and suffer through all my emotions 100% sober. And so reluctantly, that's exactly what I did.

I set a goal to stay completely sober for one month. I know that doesn't sound like a long time, but to me it felt like an eternity. In the ten years prior,

I hadn't gone without a drink for longer than a week. So that month was life changing.

Don't get me wrong; it sucked ass. It was boring as hell, and all I could think about was getting shitfaced to deal with my anxiety. The first couple weeks of sobriety were the absolute worst. I had nothing to look forward to on the weekends. I didn't want to go out because I felt like I'd be disappointing my friends if I wasn't my usual "party-mode" self. I'd grown so accustomed to the feeling of getting fucked up, it had become engrained into who I was. It was my way of rewarding myself for making it through another day. Without drugs and alcohol, where was I supposed to experience any kind pleasure in life? Where was I supposed to get my easy dopamine hit? Sobriety was not going to be a walk in the park.

But I kept reminding myself how much worse it would be if I gave in to the temptation. How awful I would feel letting an entire day go to waste, bingeing junk food alone in my room on a beautiful Saturday afternoon, then going back to sleep with the curtains completely drawn. How much money I was wasting on a $100 bag of coke that only made me feel more anxious and depressed. How much I was disappointing the greater part of me that knew I was capable of so much more.

So I took it one day at a time; not focusing on the weeks ahead, just the next 24 hours. Slowly but surely, being sober gave me the clarity I needed to focus on getting better. When I was finally ready to have a drink again, I went into it with a much more positive outlook, and I was able to manage my post-drinking "hangxiety" much more effectively. I've maintained moderation and a healthy attitude towards alcohol ever since, and I don't fuck with the yayo anymore. But for some people even one drink/toke is a slippery slope that can re-introduce bad habits, and it's best to just go cold turkey. You have to figure this out for yourself or get support to help guide you.

Whatever your relationship with drugs and alcohol is, I sincerely encourage you to go on a detox for as long as you can; whether it's one week or one month, just set a *realistic* goal that will challenge you, *commit* to it, and then achieve it. It's not easy, but I know you have the discipline and determination to make a positive change—and you will.

Practice sobriety regularly whenever your mind and body tell you that you need it. It's one of the best things you can do for yourself.

Benders are for pretenders.

Write five dope things about your life now that you're single:

#1: _____

#2: _____

#3: _____

#4: _____

#5: _____

BREATHING EXERCISE

1 Get comfortable.

2 Inhale through your nose for a **count of four.**

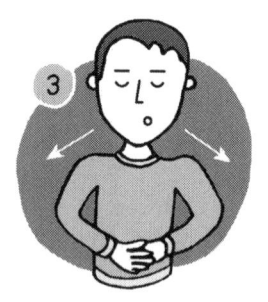

3 Hold your breath for a **count of seven.**

4 Exhale slowly through your mouth for a **count of eight.**

Repeat 10 times.

What advice would you give to your "10 years younger" self?

Take a day off to reset, recharge your batteries, and focus on your mental health. Do whatever that means to you.

World Mental Health Day is every year on **October 10**.

Personal Mental Health Day is every fucking day.

What actions can you take to boost or at least stabilise your mental health? I know I've been giving you clues; now's your chance to listen to what your inner wisdom is telling you.

#1:

#2:

#3:

#4:

#5:

#6:

#7:

#8:

#9:

#10:

Write a letter to your dad:

Three big goals

Write three goals for the next year. Under each goal, write down the steps it'll take to get there. Don't be afraid to dream big.

Tear this page out and post it somewhere you'll see it every day.

GOAL #1: _____

    STEP: _____

    STEP: _____

    STEP: _____

    STEP: _____

    STEP: _____

GOAL #2: _____

    STEP: _____

    STEP: _____

    STEP: _____

    STEP: _____

    STEP: _____

GOAL #3: _____

    STEP: _____

    STEP: _____

    STEP: _____

    STEP: _____

    STEP: _____

Is being single really the worst thing for you right now?

Hear me out. You have two things that a lot of people in relationships don't have but wish they did:

Time to focus on yourself.

Freedom to do whatever you want with your time.

These are priceless gifts. Do not take them for granted. You have all the time in the world to eventually meet *your person* and settle down, but you might only have a small window left to be single, so enjoy it!

Write down 10 things you have the **time** and **freedom** to do now that you're single:

#1:

#2:

#3:

#4:

#5:

#6:

#7:

#8:

#9:

#10:

Just a friendly reminder:

When ya look good, ya feel good.

Put on a dope outfit today, even if you're just working from home. Looking and feeling your best will have a positive impact on your mental approach to the day.

If you don't have one, treat yourself to something that makes you feel like the main character (fuck it, you deserve it).

When you're working on continuously improving yourself, it gets lonely.

When you wake up to no good morning <3 text, it gets lonely.

When you take the metro to work every morning, it gets lonely.

When you work from home and literally have not interacted with another human-being in person in over a week, it gets lonely.

When you scroll through social media and see that funny video, it gets lonely.

When you celebrate literally any holiday, it gets lonely.

When you drive by that restaurant you both loved, it gets lonely.

When you cook dinner and eat alone in front of the TV night after night, it gets lonely.

When you bury yourself in work and study and gym to keep your mind occupied, it gets lonely.

When you cab home late after a fun night out with friends, it gets lonely.

When you listen to that new album by that artist whose concert you went to together, it gets lonely.

When you're the 3rd, 5th, or even 7th wheel, it gets lonely.

When you start casually dating again and realize this new person actually SUCKS and you miss your ex more than ever, it gets lonely.

When you go to bed every night but still sleep on one side of the bed because the other side was always "their side," it gets lonely.

When you experience any kind of pleasure or happy moment without them by your side, it gets lonely.

Healing gets lonely.

. . . and that's OK.

DAY OF GRATITUDE

Write down five things you're grateful for today:

#1: _____

#2: _____

#3: _____

#4: _____

#5: _____

Write down five things you will NOT tolerate from your partner in your next relationship:

🚩 #1 _____

🚩 #2 _____

🚩 #3 _____

🚩 #4 _____

🚩 #5 _____

One of the worst things you can do is ignore the red flags and jump back into a relationship with the same type of toxic energy that broke you the first time. Respect yourself, your boundaries, and what you require when it comes to dating and healthy relationships.

On your ex moving on . . .

At some point, we all have to come to terms with the fact that our exes, just like us, are going to move on to someone else (maybe they already have).

At first that thought fuckin' suuuucks. I couldn't stand to picture my ex being intimate with someone else, physically or emotionally. I don't even know which one hurts more. They're both painful in their own way. It drove me crazy and always put me in a terrible headspace. But here are some things to remember every time those thoughts pop into your head.

1) Being in a relationship doesn't automatically equate to happiness. If your ex is already in a new relationship, it doesn't mean they're happy. If they've moved on this quickly, they likely haven't taken the time to reflect, heal, and confront their own insecurities, which means they're someone else's problem now.

   You have no clue what your ex's new situation is, and to dwell on such things is a waste of time and energy. Jumping into a new relationship right after a breakup is one of the easiest ways to cope with loneliness; anyone can do it. The right thing to do, which is of course the path less travelled, is to endure this difficult phase of your life and *figure out how to be happy on your own before you start dating again.*

   Is it going to get lonely? Yes. Is it going to suck sometimes to see other people in happy, committed relationships? Yes. Is it going to feel like you're totally stagnant because your ex has already moved on and you're still single? Yes! But your relationship status is not an indication of whether you're progressing or prospering in life. Once you get through this period, I promise you'll come out stronger, more confident, grateful, and ultimately happier with every aspect of your life—and better prepared for your next relationship.

2) At the end of the day, you and that person are no longer together, so what or who your ex chooses to do is no longer your concern. Your main focus now is to be selfish as fuck. Work on your personal growth and improve yourself every single day—period.

3) This one's tough, but maybe a small part of you can actually be happy for them. I know it seems like ages ago, but there was a point in time when you really loved this person, and they loved you back; this is why you happen to care so much who they're with now. There's love there without a place to go. It's okay to grieve that loss while also showing compassion at the same time.

At the end of the day, remember that you were not right for them just as much as they were not right for you. Try to find some empathy in the fact that, just like you, they're also trying to be happy, and you can wish them well on that journey.

4) If your ex cheated on you and now they're dating the person they cheated on you with, forget everything I just said above and FUCK 'EM. Just be glad that *you dodged a bullet* and they're someone else's problem now.

Why is it that we always associate the words "single" and "alone" together? Why do we automatically assume they go hand-in-hand? Why have we collectively bought into this idea that if we're not in a serious relationship, it means we're "alone"?

Being single doesn't mean you're alone. You have so many relationships in your life that demand your love and attention, and that nurture you and uplift you, including your friends and family. So many beautiful, wonderful, and amazing people right in front of you to fill your life with everything your heart needs to feel complete.

Most importantly, don't forget about your relationship with yourself. Cliché, I know. But why wouldn't you give yourself the same amount of love and energy that you'd give to someone else? Go and love yourself – Justin Bieber said so. Romanticize your life; take yourself out on a date. Do all that shit. Learn to do it by yourself. Once you start *really* loving all of you, you'll never *need* anyone again.

Life isn't a race to see who settles down, gets married, and has kids first...

If you've bought into this mentality, respectfully, you're doing it wrong. You've given away all your autonomy to live your life in the present moment. When you're so focused on that end goal and your position in the race, you stop enjoying all the great moments happening to you in the present. This breakup doesn't put you "behind" in life. You have plenty of time for the marriage and kids thing, if that's what you want. Be kind to yourself and allow yourself to move at your own pace.

I know lots of couples who got married and had kids late into their 30s, even 40s, and they're happier than ever.

Marriage is not the be-all, end-all. If you want to do it, great – take your time. And remember that getting married and having kids is not a requirement for a happy and fulfilling life. Don't put so much pressure on yourself.

There is no end goal. There just *"is"*.

BREATHING EXERCISE

① Freestyle it.
Go!

What did you love about your ex?

There was a time when you had a lot of love for your ex. They had qualities that you absolutely adored. You shared moments together that brought you both immense joy and happiness. That's where the sense of loss comes from: someone that you cared deeply about is no longer present in your life.

But getting over your ex doesn't mean you need to completely delete those memories from your hard drive. They're all part of your story. Whether intentionally or not, they made you a more complete, well-rounded person. So instead, use those memories to gain compassion, gratitude, and some form of closure. If you can reframe the way you think about your ex and the relationship, it'll help you let go of any bitterness and anger that you might still hold against them.

The fact of the matter is, it's not just that they weren't right for you. You weren't right for them, either. But that doesn't mean the whole thing was a waste of time. You loved. You learned. (And will continue to learn and process this.) As you move along on your healing journey, you can remember the good times with gratitude, even as you remember the struggles.

Day of Gratitude

Write down five things you're grateful for today:

#1: _____

#2: _____

#3: _____

#4: _____

#5: _____

ON TRAVELLING...

Have you ever travelled somewhere, and it made you realize:

1) The world is actually huge. It's not really a small world after all.

2) How insignificant your problems are in the grand scheme of things ...?

Every time I travel, I'm reminded of how many amazing, beautiful, cool (and hot) people there are out there. I'd been so confined to my own little bubble for so long, and there's an entire world of people I had no idea existed, waking up to the same sunrise and walking the same earth beneath me.

If you have the money and the time, travel as soon as you can and as often as you can, because there is no better time than right now. *You may never have the opportunity to go on a big solo trip again.* Everything will change once you start dating again, believe me. The experience of travelling to a foreign place completely solo is one of the most terrifying, empowering, and rewarding experiences that life has to offer.

If you don't have the money, it doesn't need to be somewhere ridiculously far or expensive. Even just exploring your city can be an adventure. Let go of fear, get out of your comfort zone and just GO.

Hopefully by now you've started to feel at least a little bit better than when we first started this journey together.

Healing takes time. So even if it's just small bits of progress, like thinking less about your ex, or laughing a little more every day, or enjoying the other people in your life, that *is* progress, and it means you're on the right track.

Keep going because it only gets better from here. TRUSSSS ME.

THE
DISCOVERING

Cue *"Welcome Back"* by Mase

Look! Over there! Do you see it? It's the light at the end of the tunnel (ha). One of the best things about getting your heart absolutely crushed into pieces is everything you discover as you put it all back together. In doing so, you're able to regain a genuine love and appreciation for *you*; sometimes this can get lost during a relationship, especially the toxic ones. When we're deep in these kinds of relationships, it's easy to forget all the unique and beautiful qualities about us that make us... Us!"

But hopefully by now you're starting to focus a little less on your ex and a lot more on you. If you're not quite there yet, that's cool, too. Everyone heals at their own pace—so don't feel like you can't move on to the next chapter (literally and figuratively), because you can.

You *are* ready. You just don't know it yet.

We're going to shift gears in this next chapter. Let's dive deeper into self-discovery and falling back in love with the most important person who's been there for you since day one: YOU.

You are the fucking SHIT. Don't ever let anyone tell you otherwise.

List all your exes below.

In ten words or less, what's a lesson you learned about *you* from that relationship? Make it positive—don't write something like "I'll never date a goofy piece of shit again."

> Brenda, Latisha, Linda, Felicia, Dawn, Leshaun, Ines, Alicia

Ex #1: _____

  Lesson: _____

Ex #2: _____

  Lesson: _____

Ex #3: _____

  Lesson: _____

Ex #4: _____

  Lesson: _____

Ex #5: _____

  Lesson: _____

Ex #6: (sheesh) _____

  Lesson: _____

Ex #7: (Damn, son...) _____

  Lesson: _____

Ex #8: (Yo ... 8!?) _____

  Lesson: _____

Ex #9: (OK, I think I see the problem here) _____

  Lesson: _____

Ex #10: (That's enough from you today) _____

  Lesson: _____

Well, would you look at that. Now you have a beautiful list of positive takeaways from what were once seemingly bad experiences. Every single "mistake" or "failure" has been a teaching moment. Defeat teaches you many things that victory can't. And just like every other past relationship, you'll learn something incredibly valuable from this breakup too.

ON OUR PARENTS . . .

We tend to pick up both good and bad habits from relationships that we observe over the course of our lives; the first (and most impactful) usually being our parents.

My parents had a very dysfunctional marriage, to put it lightly. With a lot immigrant parents, there's an added layer of complexity because it's more than just the official title of marriage that keeps them together: it's survival. My parents had two kids, limited English proficiency, and essentially no marketable skills. So they largely depended on each other to make ends meet.

I recognized from a young age that my parents weren't super compatible, but like many Korean immigrant parents, they stayed together because they (felt they) had no other choice. My dad needed to work and bring in the dough so that my mom could raise my sister and I and take care of all the household duties. My mom worked, too, which was kind of unfair now that I think about it.

Neither of my parents were in a position to raise kids on their own, especially my dad. When I was 9, my parents split up for a summer and my mom moved to a city three hours away so she could work at my aunt's convenience store. As a selfish and immature kid, I opted to stay with my dad so I could continue living at home and be with my friends (I still hate myself for that decision).

Neither my dad nor I were prepared for how much of a void my mom left in our household once she was gone. We had no kitchenware—no pots or pans, no cups, bowls, plates, or cutlery. So my dad took me to the nearest Loblaws and we picked up two of everything; two cups, two bowls, two plates, two spoons, two forks, two knives. I sensed immediately that something was very off. I cried myself to sleep every night that I was away from my mom.

Eventually my parents caved. They knew this new situation wasn't going to work out for anyone, especially my older sister and I. So reluctantly, they decided to renew their mutually beneficial partnership.

My childhood is filled with memories of birthdays, vacations, and holidays that were completely ruined by my parents' heated arguments. I made a promise to myself that I would never scream at my partner the way my parents screamed at each other. If it ever gets to that point (hopefully never), I'd make sure my kids weren't around—that shit was traumatizing.

Most of us are blessed to be in a position where our *livelihood* doesn't solely depend on our relationship (although sometimes it may feel that way). We have the autonomy to find a partner who's compatible with our love languages, our goals and aspirations, and our overall vison for life.

Maybe your parents were like mine and didn't showcase the best blueprint for a happy marriage. But, it doesn't mean your relationship has to be that way, too. We're a new generation living in a different time, and unlike our parents, we actually have a choice; to start, to stay, and to leave. That's something to be grateful for.

A lot of the positive emotional habits I possess are from watching my parents and doing the exact opposite. I communicate, I'm affectionate, I'm vulnerable, I show gratitude, I practice patience, I listen (or at least I try my best).

One of the greatest lessons I learned from my parents is that Who *you ultimately choose as your life partner is the most important decision you'll ever make, and getting your heart broken is just a rite of passage.*

You need to go through these treacherous times to truly get to know yourself, what works for you and what doesn't. You need to know what it feels like to put your full trust in someone and have it completely backfire. You need to be overlooked, unappreciated, taken for granted. Yes, you need to make the mistake of giving your heart to someone who had no business having it in the first place.

Now that you've been through real heartbreak, you're smart enough to know that *before you make any kind of long-term commitment again, you need to take your time.* Set high standards for yourself because that's what you deserve. See what's out there. Take time to truly get to know someone.

Most importantly, never settle.

Don't ever bend to someone who makes you question their love and commitment. If they do, peace the fuck out of there.

Recognize that every single breakup you've ever been through exposed an incompatibility or a problem that you and your ex couldn't solve together. They weren't meant to ride it out with you. They were there to reveal a part of you that wasn't being fulfilled and to help you get super clear about your values, your needs, and what you really deserve in love and in life.

Tell me about your parents' relationship when you were growing up. If they're no longer together or one of them isn't around, that's OK. Just pick one of them and talk about a relationship they've been in, or are in now.

What impression did your parents' relationship(s) leave on you and the way you *experience* love?

Write 20 words to describe *you* as a partner (whatever comes to mind).

#1: _____   *#11:* _____

#2: _____   *#12:* _____

#3: _____   *#13:* _____

#4: _____   *#14:* _____

#5: _____   *#15:* _____

#6: _____   *#16:* _____

#7: _____   *#17:* _____

#8: _____   *#18:* _____

#9: _____   *#19:* _____

#10: _____   *#20:* _____

What are your three biggest insecurities?

Insecurity #1 _____

Why? _____

_____

_____

_____

_____

Insecurity #1 _____

Why? _____

_____

_____

_____

_____

Insecurity #1 _____

Why? _____

_____

_____

_____

_____

Heartbreak will leave you feeling like a shell of yourself. Your self-esteem goes out the window, until you're left with nothing but a cloud of insecurities hanging over you.

You might be asking yourself: "How/when the fuck did I become such a simpy insecure piece of shit?" You might not even remember what it felt like to be single and confident in yourself.

This is totally normal. Think about it: the one person who you thought loved you the most in the entire world after your mother, who knew you inside and out and everything you had to offer, ultimately decided, "Nah, this one ain't for me." That's a tough pill to swallow, and that kind of rejection hurts.

Your ex meant the world to you; they were one of the few people whose opinion mattered. So, when they make the conscious decision to move to their next chapter without you, you're left wondering why. Mix in a couple months of loneliness, sprinkle a few bad dates in there, and you ultimately come to the conclusion that *you* are the problem.

WRONG. Your ex was just one person, one opinion out of literally billions. I try to avoid using that analogy of "billions" because it diminishes the emotional significance that your ex played in your life. What I'm trying to say is that although their opinion was significant, it's not the only opinion that matters. Just because they couldn't fully see your value does NOT mean you are not of value.

Drizzy once said, "When a good thing goes bad, it's not the end of the world. It's just the end of a world that you had with one girl."

Don't look at this situation from the perspective of you not being enough for them or not meeting their expectations. It just wasn't the right fit for either of you.

And if you think you're the only person who has insecurities, you're wrong. Everyone has insecurities, including your ex, your worst enemy, your CEO, your Amazon delivery person, your therapist, your gym crush, everyone.

Insecurities are good. They keep us humble. They remind us that we're not perfect.

We can use some insecurities to our benefit. For example, if you're insecure about your weight, great! Get your ass to the gym and use this heartbreak as the best fucking pre-workout of your life. Nothing bad ever came from a little revenge bod.

But more important than "fixing" your insecurities by getting rid of them completely (i.e. losing weight because you think you're fat), is eliminating the power they have over us and recognizing that no matter what we do/don't do, there will always be people who vibe with us and people who don't.

I stand at a whopping 5'8." There are lots of women who would never give me the time of day because I don't meet their height requirements. And that's okay. I'm not for everyone, and not everyone is for me. I know there are plenty of big beautiful women out there who love a short king; just as there are plenty of people who enjoy a little extra tummy, a big nose, small eyes, receding hair line, hairy back, grey hair, acne face, miniature titties, thunder thighs, you name it.

There's someone out there for everyone. And there's someone out there for YOU.

Your insecurities, whether within your control or not, are part of who you are. Embrace them. Like fears, insecurities are just illusions of the mind. You can't be scared of ghosts if you don't believe in them to begin with.

What are five sexy, attractive-as-fuck qualities about you? (We comin' with that Big Dick Energy)

#1: _____

#2: _____

#3: _____

#4: _____

#5: _____

What are 10 emotional qualities that your future partner MUST have?

#1: _____

#2: _____

#3: _____

#4: _____

#5: _____

#6: _____

#7: _____

#8: _____

#9: _____

#10: _____

Day of Gratitude

Write down five things you're grateful for today:

#1: _____

#2: _____

#3: _____

#4: _____

#5: _____

What are 5 things you need to work on as a partner for your next relationship?

Oh, MY BAD, did you think we were going to go through this entire thing pretending you're the most amazing, perfect, flawless human being in the universe? Well, you're right! That's exactly what we're going to do.

However, that doesn't mean we can't squeeze in a little bit of self-improvement along the way.

Part of our healing process requires taking time to introspect on how we could have done things better. Recognize your mistakes, learn from them, and carry on. Nobody's perfect.

#1: _____

#2: _____

#3: _____

#4: _____

#5: _____

Re-discovery is important...

...But so is re-invention

RE-INVENT YOUR PHYSICAL AND MENTAL HEALTH.

If they're both shit, they can only go up from here. Be patient and give yourself time. Implement small daily habits that will help you achieve your goals. Drink more water. If you're not getting enough from your diet, take supplements and multivitamins daily. Limit your screen time. Journal. Incorporate cardio into your workouts (sweating is key). Most importantly, prioritize yourself. Put your own oxygen mask on first, then worry about others.

RE-INVENT YOUR DRIVE FOR GROWTH.

It's easy to sit around and scroll through TikTok for hours when you're sad and depressed. Choose the harder path. Choose to be uncomfortable. Dive into a class or a passion project for 6 months and come out of it with a new skill. Don't try to do too much at once, otherwise you'll end up doing nothing at all. Pick one thing, finish it, then move on to the next thing.

RE-INVENT YOUR PERSONAL RELATIONSHIPS.

As you get older, maintaining friendships becomes equally as hard as making new ones. Create a vision for how you see yourself holding space within your social circle. Which relationships are most important to you? What can you do to strengthen them? On Sunday evenings, I like to text or FaceTime at least one friend to check in and see how they're doing.

Which relationships are draining and more of a chore to maintain? Is there a need for you to step outside of your circle in order to fulfil your needs? Remember that you are *never* stuck within any particular social community (although sometimes it feels that way). If a certain group of people, or certain individuals, are not for you, you can remove yourself at any time. It's not always easy, and it might just take a little bit of stepping outside your comfort zone, but it's possible.

RE-INVENT THE WAY YOU HOLD GRATITUDE.

It can literally be for the smallest things that we take for granted every day: A warm cup of coffee on a cold winter day. An amazing shit to start your morning. A short text conversation between you and an old friend. Literally, a tree that's nice to look at. Hold space in your day to acknowledge and appreciate these moments when they happen. Eventually they add up, and you'll start to notice a complete change in your mood, your mindset, and your overall well-being.

RE-INVENT YOUR SELF-IMAGE.

Have supreme confidence in yourself to the point of borderline delusion, even if you don't believe it at first. Know that you are more than worthy of anyone's love. You are capable of anything you set your mind to. You are THAT bitch. You are HIM/HER/THEM. Whatever pronouns you go by. YOU ARE THE SHIT.

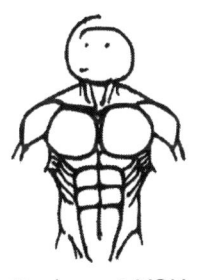

Re-invent YOU

A true partner in crime is someone who supports your goals and does everything they can to help you achieve them. They uplift you. They motivate you. They bring out the best in you.

You shouldn't have to give up your goals when someone new comes into your life. Your priorities may change, but *you* remain at the top of your priority list. Find someone who fuels and supports your aspirations, and vice versa.

Write five goals for the next year. Don't be afraid to dream big.

"But bro, you've already asked me to write out my goals like three times. Why am I doing this again?"

Great question. Goal setting is an iterative process that must be continuously repeated and manifested. Not only are we going to speak them into existence, we're going to write them—over and over again.

Now zip it and write five BIG goals for the next year:

#1: _____

#2: _____

#3: _____

#4: _____

#5: _____

DAY OF GRATITUDE

Write down five things you're grateful for today:

#1: _____

#2: _____

#3: _____

#4: _____

#5: _____

Tell me about your best friend

Bestie's Names: ....

What do you love most about them?

What's one of your favourite memories with them?

What do they love most about you?

Write a poem

(Yes, it's probably going to be absolute dogshit, but who cares.) At the very least, you'll have something to laugh about later. You don't have to share it with ANYONE like EVER but it'll be something nice and fun to come back to someday. It doesn't even have to rhyme or make sense. Just do it.

THE
HEALING

> I PRAY MY EX WILL SOMEDAY FIND TRUE LOVE AND HAPPINESS. I HOPE THEY MEET SOMEONE DESERVING OF THEIR AFFECTION, WHO CHERISHES AND HONOURS THEM EACH DAY.
>
> MY WISH FOR THEM IS TO EXPERIENCE A LOVE THAT NOURISHES THEIR HEART AND FILLS THEIR LIFE WITH WARMTH AND LAUGHTER...

...But not before me

OK, now we're talking! *Birdman hand-rub*

Congrats, my resilient friend. You've made it to the best part of the journey, the Final Frontier.

At this stage you might be waking up a little happier, maybe even excited to start the day. You feel energized and motivated. You're the most determined you've been in months. You laugh more with your friends. You're stacking your bread. For the first time in a long time, you're starting to enjoy being single and spending time alone. You have the freedom and ability to do whatever you want to do.

This is what it's all about! But it doesn't stop here. There is still more self-discovery to do. More inner peace to achieve. So let's dive *even deeper.*

Note: Just like the other chapters, it's OK if you aren't quite at this stage yet. Like I've been saying, everyone heals at their own pace.

Keep doing all the exercises we've been practicing: the breathing, the journalling, the goal setting, the gratitude. These exercises are the core foundation of your well-being. Keep going—you're doing awesome.

There is not a single person on this planet who will ever truly understand the magnitude of everything you've been through these past few months, and the mountain you had to climb to get here.

This experience is yours. It's *your* truth. It's part of *your* story.

Did it leave scars? Good. Wear them proudly. Let them serve as a reminder of all the nights you spent alone, all the pain you endured until you had the strength to get up and give yourself a second chance.

Did it almost break you? Good. It *almost* did, but it didn't. You experienced an inconceivable loss, and instead of falling into drugs, alcohol, and other choices where you could easily have lost yourself, you chose to come back home to YOU. Now you're stronger, wiser, grounded in your beliefs, and heading on to the next chapter of your life with more experience under your belt.

You've come a long way. Be proud of yourself!

My ex was the best teacher I ever had.

ON DATING AGAIN . . .

Here are three pieces of advice for if you're thinking about getting back in the dating game:

1. DATING APPS ARE REALLY FUN... UNTIL THEY'RE NOT

"OMG I looove dating apps. They're so fun and wholesome, and they make me feel so good about myself. You're totally missing out!"—said NO ONE EVER.

I've always had a love-hate relationship with dating apps. To me, they just seem a little too artificial. Maybe I'm just old-school, but whatever happened to introducing yourself at a bar? Or meeting at a mutual friend's birthday party? Listen, I get it; it's hard to meet people these days, especially if the majority of your friends are all in relationships. Plus, you probably already know 90% of the people in your social circle and the next degree out. Dating apps are convenient. Not to mention, it's hella exciting when you get a notification that someone liked you. That dopamine rush is real (and addictive.)

If you're going to get on the apps, whether it's Hinge, Tinder, Coffee Meets Bagel, Grinder, Christian Mingle, Women Behind Bars (yes, it's a thing), have fun, but also manage your expectations. Everyone's experience with dating apps will vary based on different factors, including gender, age, status, race, and mainly, how hot you are (or your proficiency with Photoshop).

First things first, let's just call it like it is. Hot people get more likes, and in turn, more matches (duh ... they're hot). Us regular-folk have to put in way more work. We can't be putting up pics of ourselves holding a giant bass from the boys' fishing weekend, or the classic from-behind shot of us on a canoe in Banff, or make extremely thought-provoking prompts about whether pineapple belongs on pizza. We don't have that luxury.

Luckily, today's apps give you more opportunities to show off your *personality*. Brains. Sense of humor. All that good stuff. And if you're one of the *uglies* who's been able to curate an intriguing dating profile that gets you matches, good on you! But that's only half the battle.

Simply put, apps are just not an ideal place for authentic connection. One "wrong move," one misinterpreted statement or emoji, and the person you've been talking to for the last three weeks can ghost you without any explanation. Why? Because they don't owe you shit. You're not a real human being (yet). You're just a little icon on the screen. Why would they waste their time explaining anything when they have five (probably more) other options right at their fingertips?

The result is *you* meticulously drafting messages with a team of writers (your best friends who have zero game but are all of a sudden experts in the art of seduction), while also throwing up emotional guardrails out of fear of abandonment and rejection. You can't expect to make authentic connections when no one is being their authentic selves.

It's become the norm in our society that if you're single, you're supposed to be on the apps. But so many people are only on the apps because they have FOMO or they think if they're NOT putting themselves out there, they're wasting their single years away. Ask ANYONE on the dating apps, and not a single one of them will tell you, "You're missing out."

In reality, everyone is talking to the same people, banging each other, going on four dates in the same week, and somehow expecting to make meaningful connections. The modern world of dating apps is such an unnatural experience. Human beings aren't built for this—and this is why they can be harmful to our mental health.

Listen, I'm not saying you should avoid apps entirely because, of course, there are LOTS of success stories, too. At the end of the day, the wider you cast your net, the higher your chances for success. But don't act surprised if you collect a bunch of sand and rocks in the process. Dating apps will drain you and burn you out over a long period. Don't get sucked into them. Take breaks, prioritize your mental health, and always remember that how you "perform" on these apps has nothing to do with you or your value.

2. YOUR FIRST FEW DATES ARE PROBABLY/DEFINITELY GONNA SUCK

So, you're ready to start going on in-person dates. Great! That's a big step, and I know it can be nerve-wracking. Just like the apps, manage your expectations when it comes to dating (in other words, keep them very low).

You're about to meet someone completely new for the very first time in a while. For me, this was terrifying. If you and your ex were together for a long time, you might still be accustomed to certain aspects of that relationship, like an inside joke, shared perspective, or even random stuff like your taste in food.

Overall, the main thing you're going to be missing is familiarity and the comfort of being able to relax and be yourself. But here's a tip: you should do that regardless—just be yourself. Go into the date with an open mind, and remember that this is a new person with some traits and quirks that might *feel* a little bit outside of your comfort zone. Embrace them, be open to them, and hopefully they'll do the same.

But fair warning: Once you get back into the dating life, there's a good chance you'll go on a bunch of dates that suck ass. We've all experienced or heard of those first date horror stories. They're either catfishes, in love with themselves, obnoxious AF, flopping on you last minute, or all four.

If there's one thing I know, it's that back-to-back-to-back shitty dates can be really discouraging and leave you second-guessing yourself. Naturally, you're going to miss aspects of your old life because, well, why wouldn't you? Your natural inclination might be to reminisce on all the good times when you were in a relationship. But don't forget to remember the bad times, too. The times when you were absolutely miserable and wanted out; the times when your ex made you feel even lonelier than you do now. Your mind is playing tricks on you; don't fall for them.

Anything worthwhile takes time. Your intention going into a first date shouldn't be to walk away with "the one." There's no need to put so much weight on a single date, let alone on a person who doesn't even know you. The goal is to have fun and live in the present moment. Simple as that. If it leads to something bigger, that's a bonus. At the very worst, you'll have a good story to tell and hopefully get a decent meal out of it.

If your dating life starts to take a toll on your mental peace, or if you're constantly comparing your dates to your ex, or obsessively checking your apps all the time, you might want to reassess whether you're ready to start actively dating again. It's OK if you're not. Go at your own pace.

3. DON'T IGNORE RED FLAGS

This is literally the simplest one but also the one we have the hardest time with. Why?

Well, because we have good intentions and want to give everyone the benefit of the doubt. We're finally getting a fresh start. As our newly single-and-ready-to-mingle selves, we want to be open to new people, perspectives, opinions, and experiences. That's how we can move on from our past life.

But moving on from your past life does not mean moving on from your core values and the things that you hold true to yourself. There's a difference between being open to new things vs. ignoring straight up red flags.

If your gut is warning you that someone is displaying a red flag or behaviour that's not for you, *trust it*. This doesn't mean immediately run away and ghost them. But as soon as you spot it, take some time to observe if it's actually true. If it is true, trust your gut, and peace the fuck out of there. It's not your job to fix someone, especially at this stage in your life.

Don't go down the path of ignoring the red flags just because they have a couple good qualities that you like (especially just great sex. Seriously, snap out of it you horny devil.) *A few good qualities will never cancel out the bad ones.* You owe it to yourself to find someone who ticks most (if not all) the boxes you've set for yourself. It might take some time, but I promise you, it'll be worth the wait.

Money actually does buy happiness when you spend it on others.

Use your money to do something nice for someone today. It doesn't have to be big. It can be as little as a cup of coffee, or a sweet little card showing appreciation to a friend.

Day of Gratitude

Write down five things you're grateful for today:

#1: ....

#2: ....

#3: ....

#4: ....

#5: ....

What are 10 things (big or small) that make you really happy?

#1: _____

#2: _____

#3: _____

#4: _____

#5: _____

#6: _____

#7: _____

#8: _____

#9: _____

#10: _____

So, I don't know if this is obvious, but you should incorporate all of these things into your life as much as possible. Take the necessary steps to fit them into your schedule on a weekly basis.

Write a letter to your mom:

What will you do differently in your next relationship?

Take a photo of this page and send it to three people:

I LOVE YOU, BITCH ♥♡

...have a nice day

(Disclaimer: don't send this to your grandma)

*D*AY OF GRATITUDE

Write down five things you're grateful for today:

#1: ....

#2: ....

#3: ....

#4: ....

#5: ....

Soul-O Activities

#1:
Grab a mat/towel and lay in the sun because a little vitamin D goes a long way.

#2:
Go for daily walks because your mind needs a recharge.

#3:
Get a kick-ass workout because sweating will immediately make you feel better.

#4:
Read a book outside because it'll take you to a new world.

#5:
Clean your house/apartment because you're a grown adult and you should do that anyways, you filthy animal. And you'll feel nice being in a clean and tidy space.

#6:
Learn a new instrument because you just never know when you'll need to bust that out.

#7:
Take a local class (pottery, cooking, a language—the one they speak in the country you most want to visit, shoe design, rock polishing, tango, martial arts ... whatever) because knowledge is power.

#8:
Redecorate your place because it's an extension of you.

#9:
Journal because therapy is too expensive.

#10:
Learn a new recipe because there's nothing sexier than someone who can throw it down in the kitchen.

#11:
Go to the movies by yourself because why the hell not?

#12:
Become a plant mommy/daddy because it's like having a kid but you won't get in trouble when it dies.

#13:
Start a home DIY project because this will inevitably happen after age 30 anyways.

#14:
Start a side hustle because who hates more money?

#15:
Crack open some wine and binge a show because who needs company when you can mind your own business and enjoy being in the comfort of your home?

Tell me about *the one that got away* (not your ex):

Six months of consistency and focus can change the trajectory of the rest of your life. Write down three goals for the next six months. They can be related to your career or your personal life—anything!

Use the **SMART** principles and create goals that are:

Specific – Measurable – Attainable – Realistic – Time-Bound

#1: _____

#2: _____

#3: _____

#4: _____

#5: _____

Now commit! There is no better time than now.

Where's your next travel destination? Why there?

_____

_____

_____

_____

_____

_____

_____

Imagine yourself there right now. Where are you *exactly*, and what are you doing?

_____

_____

_____

_____

_____

_____

_____

Manifest and make this trip happen. Start immediately. Put away literally any amount you can right now, even $5. Just start saving and keep going.

I just want to say, you've done so amazing and you deserve ALL your flowers. I'm so fucking proud of you, seriously. I know it probably doesn't come naturally, but you should be proud of yourself, too.

Write five things you're incredibly proud of yourself for since the breakup:

#1: _____

#2: _____

#3: _____

#4: _____

#5: _____

Write 10 things you want to thank your ex for:

THANK YOU, PEACE OUT

#1: _____

#2: _____

#3: _____

#4: _____

#5: _____

#6: _____

#7: _____

#8: _____

#9: _____

#10: _____

DAY OF GRATITUDE

Write down five things you're grateful for today:

#1: ....

#2: ....

#3: ....

#4: ....

#5: ....

Write a letter to your future self 10 years from now.

What have you learned about yourself through this journey?

JHEEEEEEEZ! You made it!!! You're here!

See? That was easy, right? (kidding)

Hopefully you've figured it out by now, and if you haven't, let me fill you in. This journey was NEVER about getting over your ex.

It was about *you*—returning back home to *you*.

It was about rediscovering the parts of you that you'd forgotten about: the best friend, the son/daughter, the artist, the athlete, the foodie, the gamer, the chef, the wine/whiskey connoisseur, the neat-freak who's borderline OCD, the fashion-icon, the beautiful human that lights up every fuckin room.

It was about remembering that you were a dope-ass motha fucka before them, and you will continue to be that dope-ass motha fucka after them. You are still *that* bitch, only harder, better, faster, stronger.

I hope you can look back on this last relationship now, not with bitterness, anger, or resentment in your heart, but with *gratitude*. Regardless of how long the relationship was or how badly it may have ended, it was one of the most important chapters of your life, and it was the prequel to the best chapters ahead. For a moment, even if brief, that person gave you a wonderful gift that only a select few people will ever give you in your lifetime: the feeling of being loved by another, and the opportunity to love them back.

Our exes were, and will always be, our greatest teachers. They teach us what love *is*. They empower us to realize our worth and our potential. I will be forever grateful for that.

As this chapter of your life comes to an end, another is just beginning.

So where do we go from here? Well, you may go on to find the love of your life and live happily ever after. Or you might even go through another heartbreak or two. None of us can be certain what the future holds. But what I can guarantee is that just like this breakup or any other future breakup you might experience, you will *always* come out of it as a better version of yourself.

Every adversity you face will continue to refine and enrich your character. No matter what obstacles life throws at you, you have the strength and resilience to come out on top, just as you have today.

The journey does not end here. I hope you will continue to self-discover and fill every moment of your life with boundless love and acceptance. Your relationship with yourself is the single most important relationship you will ever have. So be kind to yourself, and always remember the tremendous strides you've taken to get here.

Lastly, always believe in your worth and never settle for anything that falls short of it.

Continue to love wholeheartedly and live without regret.

I'm wishing you an abundance of wealth, excellent health, GREAT sex, uncontrollable laughter, beautiful memories, cherished moments, and most importantly: *true love.*

God bless you, you beautiful human. Now get out there and have a great fucking life.

Take care.

About the Author

Ben is a former Torontonian now living in Montreal, QC with his smoking hot girlfriend, Julia.

In his spare time, he struggles to learn French, loves to drink soju and eat Korean BBQ, and spit flamethrowing sprinkler setting rap bars for his friends.

This is his first book.

* * * * *

If you loved this book, and you feel a lot better than when you cracked open the first page, how about heading over to Amazon and leaving a 5-star review? Hint, hint. Do it.

Or buying it for a friend? (Make sure they're broken up first.)

Or sending me a DM saying: "Hey, Ben, I loved your book, you totally saved my ass, and I'm inviting you to my wedding."

On a serious note, I'm truly grateful that you allowed me to be part of your journey. From the bottom of my heart, thank you.

TikTok: soju_knows

Email: benjaminihn10@gmail.com

Made in the USA
Middletown, DE
06 June 2024